SPORTING
SUPERCARS

JEREMY WALTON & LAURIE CADDELL

SPORTING

SUPERCARS

EDITED BY KEVIN BRAZENDALE & IAN WARD

Macdonald Illustrated

Page 1 Renault's Alpine GTA, known simply as a Renault GTA in Britain

Pages 2 & 3 Motor racing connections are reflected in the UVA M6 GTR's unusual doors and one-piece rear bodywork

Left De Tomaso's venerable Pantera, shown here in its latest GT5-S guise, with rear wing and smooth body sides

Pages 6 & 7 The elegant lines of the Aston Martin are enhanced in this convertible Vantage Volante version

A **Macdonald Illustrated** BOOK
This edition first published for Marks & Spencer plc in 1988 by Macdonald & Co (Publishers) Ltd A member of Maxwell Macmillan Pergamon Publishing Corporation Reprinted for Marks & Spencer plc in 1989
Reprinted by Macdonald Illustrated in 1990
A division of Macdonald & Co (Publishers) Ltd
Orbit House
1 New Fetter Lane
London EC4A 1AR

British Library Cataloguing in Publication Data
Walton, Jeremy 1946–
    Sporting supercars.
    1. Sports cars
    I. Title   II. Caddell, Laurie
629.222

ISBN 0-356-19582-1

Printed in Yugoslavia by
Mladinska knjiga

CONTENTS

FOREW

What is a sports car? To some, it has to be a convertible, a wind-in-the-hair suntrap with minimal space but maximum agility and appeal. To others it's a saloon car that has been modified to endow it with much improved road manners. Then there are those for whom a real sports car is one in which high performance and standard-setting handling prowess are its *raison d'être*.

The term sports car is nearly as old as the automobile itself, having been coined just after World War I. 'Supercar' is a more recent description and so far has been confined in its use, implying something very special in the way of performance.

And that is what *Sporting Supercars* is concerned with. The thirty-six cars described and depicted in these pages differ radically from each other in many ways, but all have one very important common link: they have been designed and built with speed as a paramount consideration.

Some, such as the Aston Martin, the Ferraris, the Lamborghinis, the Lotus and the Porsche, are very firmly in the realms of exotica, while others, such as the humble Caterham Seven and the three-

ORD

wheeled Triking, are more akin to engines and seats on wheels. Then there are a number of 'homologation specials', cars like the RS200 and RS500 Fords, the MG Metro 6R4 and Peugeot 205 T16 built for public consumption only to satisfy the production demands of various branches of motor sport.

There are even some component-based specials, the Transformer and the UVA, for instance, whose quality lifts the kit car industry on to a new plane.

And these are all road cars of today. They are neither pipe dreams nor museum pieces. Even classics like the AC Cobra, the Ford GT40 and the Jaguar D-type are back on the road. Perhaps not known as supercars in their day, they were certainly all instrumental in the invention of the term.

My work regularly affords me the privilege of driving glorious machines like these. They call it a labour, but it is never more than a labour of love. To behold such automotive jewels is pleasure enough; to drive them is a sheer joy. If this book communicates just a fraction of that joy then it has done its job well.

Ian Ward
Editor, *Performance Tuning & Sports Car*

AC

ACE
AC

Renewing an earlier association with Ford, AC Cars' new Ace debuted its suave aluminium lines on the vast Ford stand at the autumn 1986 International Motor Show in Birmingham, where it attracted favourable attention. Its

harmonious lines and advanced four-wheel-drive (4WD) specification used many Ford components, including a choice of V6 or turbo-16-valve Cosworth power.

At that time there were no firm production plans and the two companies were not linked, but,

by the close of 1987, all that had changed. Hot on the heels of its September buyout of Aston Martin, Ford acquired a controlling 50.96 per cent of AC Cars at a reported cost of £1.3 million.

In December 1987 Ford announced it would spend an additional £5 million on building

a 90 000 sq ft factory on the Brookland Industrial Estate, near Byfleet in Surrey. This was to be for the use of AC Cars and its associate company Autokraft, which manufactures the only Ford-authorized AC Cobra and also produced the 1986 Ace prototype. Autokraft is both owned and managed by Brian Angliss, who also manages AC Cars.

The 1986 Ace was a sensuously styled targa-top two-seater that reflected the input of Ford European Design Group employees. Their beautifully proportioned machine was complemented by Autokraft's craftsmanship, so the car always looked a production possibility, even when its future was far from fixed.

The two-plus-two targa body was shown with frameless door windows and used eight pressed-alloy outer panels; the lift-off roof panel was displayed in translucent polycarbonate. Composites were used to provide front and rear crash pads on energy-absorbent telescopic rams and there was also an integral roll cage, suggesting that the car could sell in America. The wide use of composites for sill panels and internal body components contributed to the low, 2000 lb (909 kg), kerb weight that was quoted.

Built on a 97.5-inch (2476 mm) wheelbase, the Ace show car looked far longer than its actual 156 inches (3962 mm). Height was a fashionably minimal 46 inches (1168 mm), while width was 71.5 inches (1816 mm) up front and 70 inches (1778 mm) aft. In contrast, the front track, on the Ford-patterned 7 x 16-inch aluminium alloy wheels, was 2 inches greater at the front than at the back. Tyres could come from Pirelli (P700) or Goodyear (Eagle NCT), with chunky 225/45 low-profile VR casings.

To provide the anticipated 140 mph minimum level of

performance, the Ace was specified with the Ford 2.8-litre V6 of the period. This had the advantage of being already hitched up to a sophisticated 4WD system, but engineering work carried out later made it technically possible for AC to offer the torquier 2.9-litre V6 seen in the more recent Scorpio-Granada range. If indeed this engine is used in the car, which is scheduled for production in late 1988 or early 1989, the Ace will ally 150 bhp at 5700 rpm with 172 lb ft of torque at 3000 rpm.

The cast-iron 60-degree vee should allow such a light car to reach 60 mph in less than 7 seconds. To give the kind of speed suggested by the cowled-headlamp lines, AC Cars also examined the installation potential of the engine used in the Ford Sierra RS Cosworth saloons.

This four-cylinder unit is topped by Cosworth's aluminium cylinder head. It packs turbocharging, double overhead camshafts and sixteen valves into a 2-litre

Top The Ace show car of 1986 was powered by Ford's 2.8-litre V6. Production should see the 2.9-litre V6 or possibly the 204 bhp Cosworth twin-cam used

Right Much of the interior is sourced from the Ford Granada/Scorpio powerhouse that is based on the Ford Sierra's iron cylinder block.

The performance potential of the 4WD Ace is startling, for the Ford-Cosworth turbo motor generates 204 bhp and more than 200 lb ft of torque. In a comparatively weighty Sierra, that is enough genuinely to exceed 145 mph and to return a 0-60 mph time of 6 seconds. Thus

a 'Cosworth Ace' has the potential to travel beyond 150 mph with appropriately demonic acceleration.

Much of the 4WD system is along proven Scorpio/Sierra lines, but 'the engine is set sufficiently far back in the chassis that the front drive shafts do not bend to pass through its sump', say Ford.

As in the Ford saloons, epicyclic gearing is used to split power delivery at the rate of thirty-four per cent front and sixty-six per cent rear. Both the central and rear differentials employ Ferguson patent viscous couplings, limited-slip devices which rely on the viscosity of fluid in association with multiple 'clutch' plates for

The performance potential of the 4WD Ace is startling, for the Ford Cosworth turbo motor generates 204 bhp and more than 200 lb ft of torque

their operation. An alternative to the previously more popular mechanical devices, using gear systems or clamping plates, the viscous coupling is currently employed in 4WD systems as diverse as those of BMW, Volkswagen, Lancia and Honda, plus many Japanese prototypes.

As was the case for the original Panther Solo, the chassis of the show Ace was the work of former Ford USA designer and contemporary consultant, Len Bailey. It comprised a very strong steel monocoque and all-independent suspension. At the front this took the form of a wishbone with lower trailing link, while at the rear Ford's predilection for MacPherson struts was exploited. Many of the rear suspension components were drawn from the Escort RS Turbo.

Ride height and the front shock absorber and coil spring unit's damping characteristics were adjusted, and a front anti-roll bar was provided. Rack-and-pinion steering, without power assistance, was planned, along with the Ford Scorpio's adjustable top column, which served both

Right Low-profile Goodyears on striking five-spoke alloy wheels fill every inch of the Ace's rear wheel arches

Left Four small Hella headlights are neatly faired into the nose of the Ace

Below The Ace's truncated rear is reminiscent of the latest TVR line, although more rounded and graceful

rake and reach functions.

The use of internal Ford components extended to the cockpit's Scorpio-Granada fascia, dashboard layout, instrumentation and heated windscreen. Ford also supplied the electrical wiring loom and systems to support these components. Recaro sports seats supplied a sporty tone to the cabin, which featured twin door mirrors.

Incidentally, AC first coined the Ace name in the 1930s when it made its own engine, but the cars made between 1953 and 1963 used either Bristol's version of the pre-war BMW in-line six or a Ford straight-six.

Usually known as the AC 2.6, or Ace-Zephyr, the Ford unit, modified by Ruddspeed of Sussex, was taken from the Zephyr saloon and uprated to produce a maximum of 170 gross bhp at 5500 rpm from its 2553 cc. Not many such Aces, or close cousin Acecas were made because keeping abreast of the demand for the V8 Cobra took up all the capacity of the then Thames Ditton-based company.

From its neatly integrated quartet of Hella headlamps to its shining five-spoke wheels, the new AC Ace promises honourably to sustain the reputation of those earlier cars.

A C

COBRA

AUTOKRAFT

The post-war austerity of Britain made for economy motoring in the broadest sense of the term: not only did cars have to be frugal, but they had to be very cheap and when they were coming to the end of their useful lives they were rejuvenated as 'specials' with some kind of

lightweight body added on. This ultimately led to the birth of the kit-car industry, with countless manufacturers popping up to produce body or body/chassis kits to be powered by whatever engines were available in plentiful supply. Hence, many 1950s sports cars made do with 1172 cc of side-valve Ford. For such a poor

nation, England then had a multitude of sports cars on its roads.

AC, of Thames Ditton in Surrey, resumed their post-war production in 1947 and soon took the big step of building their own exclusive sports car. At the 1953 London Motor Show they unveiled the Ace, which was

equipped with a 2-litre, six-cylinder engine of their own design. The car was attractive, handled well and had a fair turn of speed, courtesy of its 85 bhp. Later Aces featured engines from Bristol (their six of pre-war BMW design) and Ford and the various versions were very popular.

To American Carroll Shelby, the

> *. . . it managed 60 mph (96 kph) in a shattering 4.2 secs and 100 mph (161 kph) in 9.8 secs! However, whereas the 289 Cobra was a fairly well balanced car the 427 was a pig . . .*

Ace had everything except the right performance, despite AC's experiments with tuned versions of the 2.6-litre Ford; they had even built their own flat-six motor. From Shelby's side of the Atlantic, however, there was much cheaper and more plentiful power available from the countless V8s which had to haul several tons of steel and chrome along in big saloons. Such power would give remarkable results.

Thus, 1963 saw the birth of the legendary AC Cobra, the most famous of the Anglo/American sports cars, which also included the TVR Tuscan, the Allard and the Sunbeam Tiger. AC modified their chassis a little to take the Ford 4.7-litre V8 engine, which was also to be used in the Mustang

and was fitted in America, where most Cobras were sold. This AC had astonishing performance: it was able to reach a top speed of around 140 mph and accelerate from rest to 60 mph in under 6 seconds.

By the time the Cobra came out, its chassis was already ten years old, but Shelby hadn't finished yet. He felt that more would be even better, so he fitted the big-block Ford 427 motor,

Right It's still Ford power in the latest Cobra with the current Ford US 5-litre V8 in High Output form, enough to give 140 mph-plus performance

Below One area that has changed significantly with the interior appearing far more luxurious

Right Hallibrand centre lock alloy wheels are used, shod with suitably massive tyres of 225 section at the front and even larger 255 section at the rear

which in metric terms has a whopping 7-litre capacity! *Motor* magazine tested a Cobra with a tuned 7-litre engine and it managed 60 mph (96 kph) in a shattering 4.2 secs and 100 mph (161 kph) in 9.8 secs! However, whereas the 289 Cobra was a fairly well balanced car, the 427 was very front heavy and a pig to drive; it was also, surprisingly, unreliable because of the lack of cooling air around the mighty

Far left The lines of
the Autokraft MkIV
are those of the last
of the Cobras, built
to house the massive
Ford 427 cu in (7-
litre) V8

Left . . . when 5 mph
bumpers had not
even been thought
of in the USA

power plant squeezed as it was
into the tight confines of the
engine bay. In motoring legend,
however, none of that matters a
jot, and the Cobra is the most
plagiarised car around today in a
world of replicars and pastiches.

Just like the GT40, the AC Cobra
lives on with the blessing of Ford,
who were assigned the Cobra
name from Shelby in 1965 and
who actually took over AC in 1987.
The MkIV is built by Autokraft in
Weybridge, just a few miles from
the home of the classic originals.

The MkIV is based on the later
car's chassis which housed the
mighty 7-litre motor but much of
the rest of the design has been
updated, although this has been
done without compromising the
basic specification. The chassis is
the classic ladder frame; massive
4-inch cross-braced tubes
constitute the centre section with

a smaller-diameter peripheral
framework mig-welded into
place.

The bodywork is manufactured
from 16 swg aluminium and takes
200 man hours to complete. It is
then given no fewer than fourteen
coats of paint to make sure of the
highest quality of finish. Cobra
suspension changed a lot over the
years, but the MkIV uses modern
twin wishbones with coil springs
and damper units at either end
and a sharp-reacting rack-and-
pinion steering system. To ensure
that the car stops as well as it goes,
there are large discs all round,
with those at the front ventilated,
and the car sits on Hallibrand alloy
centre-lock wheels shod with
modern Goodyear tyres of 225
section at the front and 255 section
at the rear.

The heart of any Cobra,
however, is its engine, and the

MkIV still uses a development of the small-block Ford original. When the Boss Mustang came along, its capacity went up from 289 cu in to 302 cu in, which means that it displaces some 4950 cc. With subtle tuning, this Ford V8 provides the AC with acceleration to keep it up there with the rest of the sporting supercars. A top speed of over 140 mph (224 kph) is the order of the day, with blinding acceleration which will get the 23.5 cwt (1196 kg) car to 60 mph (96 kph) in around 5.5 seconds. The MkIV really scores in its cruising ability, being fitted with a Borg-Warner five-speed gearbox instead of the four-speed original.

There have been many stories about the brutal nature of Cobra handling, and this is certainly true of the awesome 427s. However, the smaller ACs were very well balanced and the MkIV follows that tradition. With Connolly hides and Wilton carpets, the interior is plushly finished, but the car is still a roadster, with cut-down doors and the minimum of protection from the elements. The AC will not dart through high-speed corners and build up

tremendous cornering forces like a low, mid-engined supercar; it has instead the sort of handling which encourages the driver to hang one elbow out over the door and use plenty of acceleration out of tight corners to push the rear end slightly out of line. The accent is much more on fun than outright dynamic ability. And of course when the road straightens out, that throbbing V8 can be given its head to send the Cobra gobbling up tarmac at an increasingly rapid rate.

Autokraft have proved with their many orders for the MkIV from all over the world that there are those who are still willing to pay a hefty price for the finest of British craftsmanship in a package which represents the classic marriage between two automotive giants separated by the Atlantic Ocean.

ASTON

VANTAGE VOLANTE

ASTON MARTIN

The name Aston Martin conjures up visions of classic British thoroughbreds in the sporting tradition, elegant Grand Tourers and James Bond. In its history, the company (named after founder Lionel MARTIN and the success achieved at a hillclimb with an

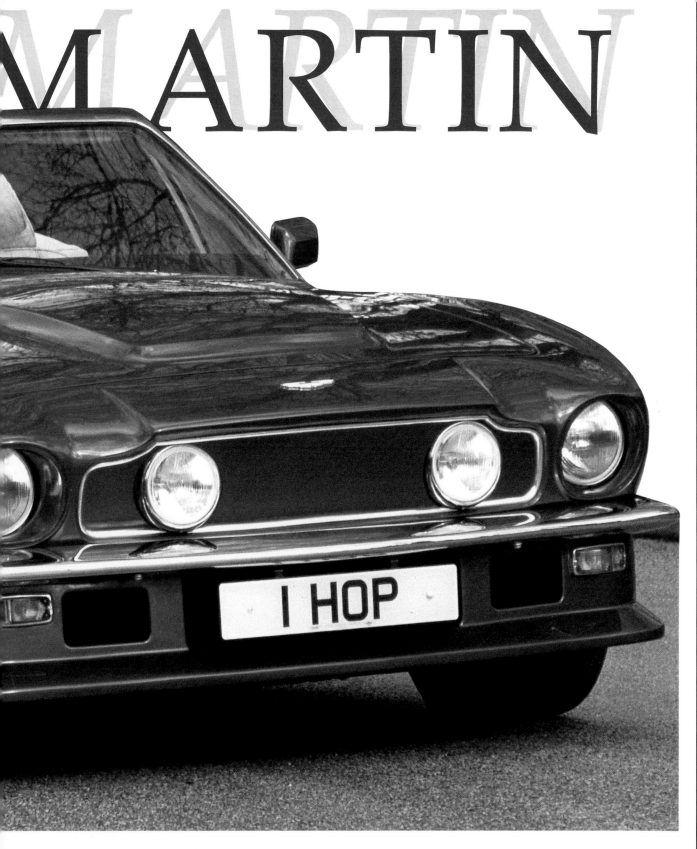

early car at ASTON Clinton) has produced some of the finest British high-class sporting cars both for road and track, where the pinnacle of its achievement was victory at the gruelling Le Mans 24-Hours in 1959 with the DBR1.

Through the 1950s, the company built some splendid roadsters in the guise of the DB series (these cars named after then company boss, Sir David Brown) and into the 1960s, the DB4s, 5s and 6s vied with Jaguar for the title of 'fastest British sports car'.

By 1970 the two marques had diverged completely, for Jaguar were well into developing their classic V12, while Aston Martin had already produced their own four-cam V8. Aware that the cars they were building at the tail end of the 1960s could no longer compete with the emergent Italian 'supercars', in terms of outright speed at least, Aston Martin took the bold step of

. . . the big Aston is race bred, with twin wishbones at the front and a de Dion tube at the rear, a semi-independent means of rear suspension once the norm

Right The blanked-off radiator grille reveals that this is the high-performance Vantage version of Aston's finest

Far right The familiar alloy V8 produces 403 bhp and a massive 390 lb ft of torque from 5.3 litres

Below right The Volante's outline is altered with the addition of a spoiler faired into the boot and side skirts

producing a completely new engine. Their gifted Polish engineer Tadek Marek set about the task with relish and came up with a 5340 cc motor which, although Aston Martin were not willing to quote horsepower

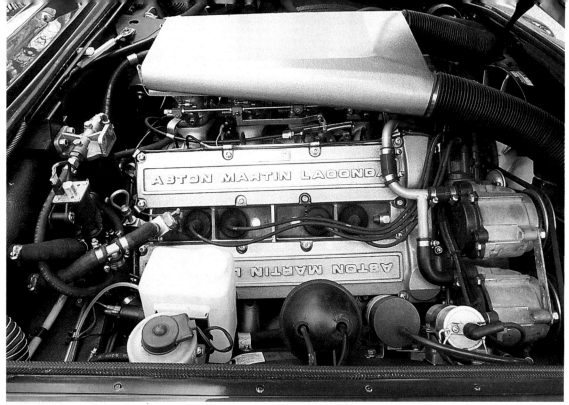

figures, probably had 300 bhp, enough to give the hefty DBS V8, into which it was fitted, a top speed of over 160 mph and acceleration from 0-60 mph of less than 6 secs. That was supercar performance in anybody's language.

Unlike some supercar rivals, the big Aston was, and still is, very much a luxury Grand Tourer with sizeable rear seats and boot, the whole car outrageously large for a two-door with a width of 6 ft, length of over 15 ft and a running weight not that far short of two tons. However, that lusty engine has never let the big Aston fall behind in terms of performance. When it looked like it, Aston Martin countered with their Vantage model with a tuned engine which probably produced nearer 350 bhp. This gave the beast a top speed of around 170 mph and enabled it to reach 60 mph in 5.4 secs. The penalty came in terms of fuel consumption, for the Vantage models were hard pressed even to make 15 mpg with gentle use!

Just as the Vantage name and improved performance sprang

from the six-cylinder models of the 1960s, so that tradition was continued when the Newport Pagnell, Buckinghamshire, company announced the Volante convertible in 1977. With a power hood which folded flat in seconds, the open-air Aston proved popular with those to whom posing on the French Riviera was as important as blasting down the autoroutes on the way there.

The combination of extra power and extra headroom came to fruition when the Vantage Volante was announced in late 1986. By this time, the company had started to quote performance figures again after a couple of decades of declining to do so due to a ridiculous escalation of quoted figures on both sides of the Atlantic. The Vantage Volante boasted some 403 bhp and 390 lb ft of torque which, if accurate, would make the engine one of the most powerful ever fitted to a road car, and who would doubt Aston Martin's integrity? If that wasn't enough, then the 'Zagato specification' engine could be ordered with some 432 bhp, but

Right The Aston's power operated hood fits snugly enough to withstand the car's prodigious top speed of over 170 mph

Below & below right Traditional materials, such as Connolly leather burr walnut and Wilton carpet are used to give an appearance more flamboyant than traditional

this would increase substantially the car's hefty £93 500 price tag!

Even the 'cooking' Vantage Volante has to be one of the world's most exotic cars, and it can be ordered with either a five-speed ZF gearbox or a Chrysler automatic. If you choose the sporting former, then your Aston should be able to exceed 175 mph and reach 60 mph in 5.2 secs.

The suspension of the big Aston is race bred, with twin wishbones at the front and a de Dion tube at the rear, a semi-independent means of rear suspension once the norm for Grand Prix cars.

The Aston has a steel platform base with a tubular steel frame clad with aluminium panels, and

these last items are lovingly created from sheet material by a dedicated band of craftsmen with skills which have largely disappeared in an age of robotised mass production. Although the main shape of the car is still recognizable as the William Towns original (still timeless after almost two decades of production) the overall look of the Aston has been spoiled somewhat by the rather tasteless wheel arch extensions to cover the 8 in x 16 in alloy wheels shod with massive 255/50 Goodyear tyres. It is more fitting for a back-street conversion than one of the most expensive cars money can buy.

That is the only glitch in the car, for the rest is as well made and as luxurious as any car on-offer, with Connolly hide for the interior and the boot, burr walnut for the dashboard and door trims, and Wilton carpet for the floor. The trim colour is matched for the hood and again for the set of luggage which is tailor made to fit the boot.

Although the monstrously powerful engine flings the Vantage Volante up the road like a lightweight, the car feels a little too large for smaller back roads. On more open terrain, however, it hustles along at enormous speed, its chassis well up to the task of coping with the prodigious performance available.

A true 'supercar', the Aston Martin Vantage Volante can turn more heads on the harbour front at Monte Carlo than most any other car, but get serious about driving and it will turn just as many heads as it roars past!

AUDI

SPORT QUATTRO
AUDI

The ultimate in Audi's quattro all-wheel-drive range is the 150 mph (240 kph) Sport coupé. Only 220 of these short-wheelbase two-plus-twos were built, fewer than ten were reserved for the UK, at a retail price of £58 500 each. Yet the Sport has a significance beyond its

motor sport purpose, pioneering the use of new materials and exploring competition horsepower levels beyond 600 bhp.

The debutant 1980 quattro coupé, equipped with 200 horsepower, won no prizes for beauty, but it set the rest of the motor business buzzing. 'Quattro' was the Italian word Audi borrowed to denote four-wheel-drive (4WD) on all relevant models and the small 'q' is of the company's choosing. The first quattro offered a top speed of 135 mph (216 kph), 0-60 mph (96 kph) acceleration in some 7 seconds, and 20-24 mpg.

Those aggressive quattro coupé lines were shortened by 12.6 inches (320 mm) for the Sport, all in the cause of rallying manoeuvrability around hairpin bends and tiny mountain tracks. The result, first shown at the 1983 Frankfurt Motor Show, was a car

Above The raised bonnet section with its minuscule air intakes indicates that this is the rare Sport quattro

even uglier than the original, but much lighter and brutally effective in the speed stakes. Even for public sale the Ingolstadt works in Upper Bavaria had extracted 300 bhp from its front-mounted five-cylinder engine, enough for the quattro to exceed 150 mph (240 kph).

The Sport brought many plastic composites into production, albeit limited production. Most of its exterior panels were made in lightweight materials, Kevlar becoming expensively commonplace in this quattro concoction. Cooling demands for a new 2.1-litre aluminium turbo-motor placed a premium on air ducting scoops, intake and grilles.

At that British price beyond £58 000 (when the original 200-horsepower model was listed at under £30 000 in 1987), only eight of the left-hand-drive (LHD) Sport quattros were officially imported.

The original production run was of 200 – the minimum number that had to be produced for the Sport to be recognized in the Group B category of the period. A further twenty competition-developed examples were also built. In 1985 Audi debuted a ferocious 'evolution' S1 version of the Sport quattro, which boasted huge spoilers, water-cooled brakes, a rear water radiator and a variety of experimental transmissions.

All Sports have unique aluminium blocks for their five-cylinder engines, in place of the quattro's usual iron and for the road these are hitched to the early Audi 4WD system, distributing power front and rear on an equal fifty-fifty basis (only since 1987 have Audis had variable power splits, courtesy of a Torsen centre differential).

Developing a KKK-turbocharged 300 horsepower from 2.1 litres involved a fundamentally new engine design, as well as the use of a larger turbocharger than the one that appeared in the original 200 bhp quattro. Instead of a single-overhead-camshaft cylinder head, Audi created a twin-cam design, with four valves per cylinder (twenty in total). Originally this engine shared many design principles with the four-cylinder, sixteen-valve unit in the Volkswagen GTi.

The winged S1 derivative, for factory rally use, was the result of even more radical development between 1984 and May 1986. At that point Audi had a reliable 450-500 bhp, enough for a car to

Right The truncated lines of the Sport quattro. Note in particular just how short is the wheelbase, shortened in the interests of making the rally car more responsive

Below An in-line five-cylinder as usual for a quattro but in this case with an aluminium block and a 20-valve twin-cam head to produce in excess of 300 bhp

sprint to 60 mph (96 kph) in 3 seconds or less. Yet that was far from the end of the Sport quattro's potential. Fitted with ever larger wings and an engine yielding 598 bhp, the S1 Sport went to the American Pike's Peak hillclimb of 1987 and beat allcomers to the 4301-metre summit, accelerating to 100 mph (160 kph) as rapidly as do the best turbocharged Grand Prix cars!

The Sport's use in top-class motor sport justified research into six-speed gearboxes, automatic five-speed transmissions and

lightweight body materials. Even the road car wore 9-inch-wide alloy wheels with very special Michelin tyres, but despite its competition origins the Sport is properly finished for road use. The leather and cloth cabin trim is in pleasantly muted greys. The back seat, however, compressed almost to the backrests of the front seats by the shortened wheelbase, is fit only for parcels and toddlers.

Instrumentation is considerably better than that of the starkly served standard product. Red needles point to a maximum of 300 kph (186 mph), and a thunderous 7400 revs are marked as the maximum on the matching tachometer.

On initial urban acquaintance the astounding Audi is not let down by temperamental behaviour. Hot or frosty cold, the

Bosch LH-Jetronic injection engine flips instantly into life.

Over level crossings, the increased stiffness of the all-strut suspension and giant (235/50) Michelin tyres is noticeable, but the five-cylinder engine rumbles flawlessly through traffic queues without so much as a hiccup. In fact only a slightly deeper note from the twin exhausts marks the presence of such amiable power.

How rapid is the standard Sport? On a German motorway one has worked up to an indicated 270 kph (168 mph) at a rousing 7200 engine revs, while *Autocar* has measured the performance of a quattro Sport accurately at 155 mph (248 kph). A standing quarter-mile can be dispensed with in some 13.5 seconds with a terminal speed of 104 mph (166 kph), and the much publicized 0-60 mph (96

Race harnesses point to the fact that this is no ordinary quattro . . . its very abbreviated nature is shown by the almost total absence of rear seats

kph) sprint takes only a scant 4.8 seconds. Fuel consumption averages 20 mpg.

But what makes the greatest impression is that unearthly quattro grip. Even when 5000 rpm is registered, the 4WD and the fat tyres slither only slightly before you engage the clutch. Hanging on for the full 7400 rpm in second brings 63 mph (101 kph), and third gear supplies closer to 100 mph (160 kph). The Sport quattro covers over 135 mph (216 kph) in fourth, before the rev-counter demands a gear-change into fifth.

If you wanted to listen to the stereo at 100 mph, you could quite easily. The Audi Sport quattro is working at 4300 rpm and 100 indicated mph (160 kph), but it is perfectly relaxing, its stability and strong engine happy to sustain 137 mph (219 kph) and 6000 rpm. The hardening exhaust and engine voices bend to your will, cruising beyond the pace of many

light aircraft.

Even at 140 mph (224 kph) you feel safe, courtesy of the enormous quadruple ventilated disc brakes, further enhanced by standard ABS anti-lock electronics from Robert Bosch. The Sport quattro boasts discs of 11.02 in (280 mm) diameter. To put that into interesting perspective, that's bigger than the wheels of the original Mini.

While 4WD mid-engined rivals have cabins reverberating to more decibels than a Majorca disco, the Audi's cockpit is not shared by its potent engine. And the quattro's four wheels are driven without the tortured transmission wailings suffered by its opponents from Peugeot, Ford and MG.

The Sport quattro is a rarity in the class of the Porsche 911, but practical for everyday use. An ugly duckling, transformed into transportation of almost magical qualities. *Wundercar!*

BMW

M3

BMW

L ike Ford's RS Cosworth, its great racing rival, the M3 version of the BMW 3-series saloon owes its existence to international motorsport regulations. The result is the fastest – over 140 mph (224 kph) – and safest (standard anti-lock braking),

production version of BMW's best-selling small saloon.

The M3 is four cylinders of fun that in its 1987 debut season scooped up the World Touring Car Championship for Drivers, the European Touring car title, and National Championships from Finland to Australia. This remarkable BMW demonstrated its versatility by winning the European Hillclimb Championship and the World Rally Championship qualifying round in Corsica, the latter the achievement of a privately financed team from Britain.

What makes the M3 such a special BMW? On paper the answer is difficult to see, for many four-cylinder BMW saloons had preceded this international winner, and some were far from fire-breathing. But that simple 'M' prefix should stand for modesty rather than motorsport, for the company's own Motorsport division engineered into this car every aspect that could effect real track performance.

BMW's aviation, marine and automotive piston engines have always been special; the M3's motor is simply more special than most. It was developed in 1981 from the M-series of six-cylinder engines mighty 24-valve units that had propelled the M1 two-seater and the M635 coupé to speeds beyond 150 mph (240 kph). The four-cylinder version kept the four valves per cylinder and dual overhead camshafts that BMW had developed for Formula II racing in the sixties and seventies, its deep-breathing aluminium cylinder head topping a tough 2302 cc iron cylinder block.

Announced in May 1986, the production M3 comes only in left-hand drive and develops 200 bhp at a rousing 6750 rpm. This is enough to achieve a claimed 146 mph (235 kph) and a sizzling 6.7-second time for the 0-60 mph sprint – a significant gain over the 130 mph (208 kph) capabilities of the previous flagship of BMW's 3-series, the 325i. Yet the factory racing models of 1987 developed up to 300 bhp at a raucous 8000 rpm, sufficient to power the brightly coloured competition cars to 60 mph in 4.6 seconds (about as quickly as a 5-litre Lamborghini V12 can manage the same sprint . . .) and nearly 175 mph (280 kph).

The M3 tag denotes much more than a replacement engine. The production models (5000 were made the first year, allowing the car to compete from March 1987 onward), feature modified bodywork, brakes and suspension.

The interior is pretty well standard BMW, except that the eagle-eyed will spot the discreet stripes of the Motorsport emblem on steering wheel, gear lever knob and seats

Below MPower and plenty of it – some 200 bhp at 6750 rpm from the 16-valve four-cylinder twin-cam

Right The plain 3-series body is dressed in untypically flamboyant fashion for BMW, with skirts and spoiler

Most obvious are the body changes, such as steel wheel arch extensions big enough to accommodate 10-inch-wide racing wheels, and larger spoilers front and rear.

Other rather more subtle modifications include a raked rear window and bootlid height raised by 1.6 inches (40 mm). The transmission remains that of an apparently simple front-engined, rear-drive saloon but the five-speed gearbox is of competition heritage and sports the usual racing shift pattern, with first on a dog leg back and to the left and the other four ratios in the conventional four-speed pattern. There is also a limited-slip differential for extra grip, and a

bigger, 15.4-gallon (70-litre), fuel tank at the rear.

Secreted under flares and spoilers are substantial changes to the steering system, including replacement stub axles to accommodate the wheel bearings of the bigger and heavier 5-series. Production M3s have power steering and suspension that is modified in all essential aspects: replacement dampers, sports springs and anti-roll bars front and rear.

Behind standard 7 x 15-inch alloy wheels, the M3 offers the public substantially larger, and thicker, disc brakes. The popular Robert Bosch anti-lock (ABS) electronic braking system has been further developed for the M3, so that it is not activated until emergency braking is needed. These modifications add enormously to the driver's appreciation of the car, as does the sympathetically shaped seating. The leather-rimmed sports

steering wheel carries the Motorsport emblem discreetly, and the fascia holds BMW's usual clear, black and white analogue instrumentation. A second glance at the instruments shows that they too have been modified: a rev-counter reading to a 7300 rpm red line, an oil temperature gauge, and a 260 kph (161.5 mph) speedometer have been introduced.

In action, the M3 has established high standards of road and track behaviour, the racer in particular shining in the performance stakes with its staggering cornering ability, joyous engine and stunning brakes. That is not to denigrate the road car, a civilized cousin that is every bit the wolf in sheep's clothing. The M3's worth can be judged from the fact that many Britons have bought examples of the car, even though the steering is on the 'wrong' side. The cars cost £23,550 apiece in the winter of 1987-8, but you could always justify the extravagance by telling people you bought it for its remarkable economy: it *could* return 48.6 mpg, if you were to stick to 56 mph (90 kph)!

B M W

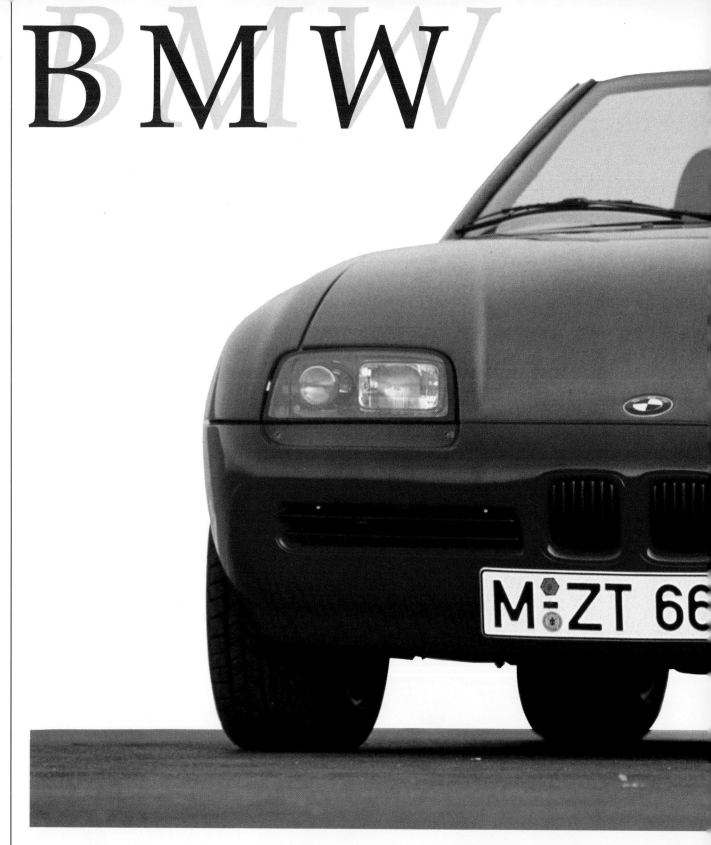

Z1

BMW

Although in the 1980s the picture conjured up in most minds by the name BMW is that of a sport saloon, the Bavarian company has built some fabulous sports cars. These include the race-winning 328 of the 1930s and the rare '50s V8s, the 507 and

the 503. The Z1 looked set to reaffirm that sporting prowess when it went into limited production during the summer of 1988.

Perhaps the most revered number in BMW's catalogue of production hits was that of the pre-war 328. That was a nimble two-seater convertible with a then uniquely smooth flow of six-cylinder power. In bare outline – soft top, six-cylinders, front engine, rear drive – the Z1 repeats the recipe, but there is absolutely nothing old-fashioned in the way that the formula is executed.

The Z1 sprang from BMW's high-tech 'think tank', BMW Technik GmbH. Just as BMW Motorsport evolved as a separate concern, looking after a specialist area for the parent company, so BMW Technik has been charged, since January 1985, with the responsibility of turning trends into reality.

The Z1 name is no accident: *Zukunft* means future in German and '1' signifies that it was the first futuristic project realized by BMW Technik. The Z1 began as a technical exercise for the 1990s, combining research into modern materials with styling by ex-Porsche designer, Harm Lagaay.

The basic layout of the Z1 is unpretentious: a production 325i six-cylinder engine sits beneath the sloping front bonnet, but its 170 horsepower hauls a scant 2420 lb (1100 kg) of advanced bodywork. Even in environmentally conscious catalytic-convertor form, this 2494 cc unit can haul the 49.1-inch (1248 mm) high Z1 to a claimed 143 mph (229 kph), completing the 0-60 mph (96 kph) run in

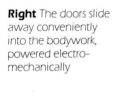

Right The doors slide away conveniently into the bodywork, powered electro-mechanically

Above The Z1 is BMW's first purpose-built convertible for very many years, since the 507 and 503 of the '50s in fact and consequently is far sportier than its converted saloons

just 7 seconds.

Fewer than 100 employees, in a modern Munich compound, were responsible for the development of the Z1 over a three-year period. The most striking features are the steel monocoque chassis, which incorporates a plastic floor and the wide use of scratch-resistant outer body panels. These emphasize low-slung speed in a comparatively stubby 154.4 inches (3921 mm) stem to stern.

The extensively used term 'plastic' covers a multitude of materials, supplied by leading specialists from all over the world. For instance, thermoplastics come from General Electric Plastics in the USA, while a sandwich section of plastics used to reinforce the main structure is supplied by Swiss firm Seger and Hoffman. Continuing the international

Short and stubby it may be, but the Z1 has a charm which is lacking in the company's saloons. Its charm doesn't detract from its capabilities, however, as the Z1 can generate an impressive 1*g* cornering force

theme, the seven-spoke 'spider's web' aluminium wheels (7.5 x 16 inches) are supplied by an Italian company and the bucket seats come from France.

The strength of the steel chassis is such that some of the development mileage was completed before the outer body panels were fitted. This internal strength ensures that the Z1 does not suffer from floppy handling or

alarming groans over bumps, as do so many convertibles.

Apart from the sleek outline essential to a sports car, the coachwork also offers an electro-mechanical system to lower and raise the side doors, although high door sills are retained to provide side protection. The effect was eerie at the car's Frankfurt public debut, but undoubtedly many customers will appreciate the extra dimension that the electric doors add to fresh-air motoring.

Aerodynamics play a large part in the development of cars today and BMW Technik did not ignore the difference between open and shut convertible airflow. An aerodynamic drag factor (Cd) of 0.42 with the hood up and 0.34 'shut' is reported, all without obvious spoilers or wings. BMW has shaped the underbody and exhaust carefully to provide some of the suction 'ground effect' that used to win races for Grand Prix Lotuses and that the English company has also endeavoured to employ on its most recent road cars.

The ease with which a convertible's hood can be raised and lowered, is paramount in bringing full enjoyment to open-air motoring and BMW employs a proven system in the shape of the complex, but effective, over-centre mechanism that appears on the 3-series convertible. Operation for the 3-series is 'finger-light' and fast, so there is no reason to think that the Z1 will not match that car in its ease of operation and freedom from annoying leaks of both water and air.

Although many 'experts' will tell you that a front engine and rear drive is old-fashioned, racing cars having preferred a mid-engined layout since the late 1950s and early 60s. But the mid-engined layout poses problems of its own, such as excessive cabin noise, excess heat and the accommodation of people and luggage. BMW has avoided the trap and provided handling that, in terms of sheer grip, compares with the best in the world. How was this impossibility achieved?

The first priority was to position that front engine as far back in the chassis as possible, and to ensure that it lay low in the engine bay. Reported weight distribution is a remarkably even forty-nine per cent front and fifty-one per cent rear. That near equality in mass was achieved by placing the fuel-injection six well behind the front axle line, canted over at an angle of 20 degrees. The water radiator and some steering components are from the luxury 7-series.

The strut front suspension draws on elements from the production 3-series, including the aluminium axle links of the M3. At the rear a completely new BMW Technik 'Z-linkage' provides lateral and longitudinal location. Judging by the amount of wheel travel provided, the Z1 will offer ride comfort as well as a reported 1g cornering capability on the generous 225/45 R16 tyres. That 1g figure is tantalizingly good: the highest figures independently recorded by *Road & Track* are 0.91g for two Chevrolet Corvettes and 0.773g for Porsche's 944.

Public reaction to pre-production publicity was so favourable that the board gave approval for the manufacture of six a day, and an official launch was held at the September 1986 Frankfurt Motor Show. Still months ahead of production, the public's delight at seeing BMW 'back in the sports-car business' was evident, and the early production run was all pre-sold, even at a predicted price of more than £23 000 each.

SUPER 7

CATERHAM

Driving a Caterham or Lotus 7 is one motoring experience not to be missed. If the weather is good enough to enjoy open-air motoring, you can be sure that no other production car will supply so much pleasure, so quickly.

While the front wings flap and you sit peering past the old-fashioned headlamps, the Seven simply gets on with the job of providing the kind of speed and exhilaration associated with two-wheeled machines, but rather more safely – it truly is the 'four-wheeled motor bike'. The fact that it is over thirty years old in concept is irrelevant when you are sitting before the responsive controls in that snug cabin.

This extraordinary device is often lumped in with the Morgan by casual onlookers: both share old-fashioned British sports-car coachwork, but both are distinctly individual characters. The Seven is the flyweight challenger with steering that responds to the slightest rim pressure; the Morgan is more solid and a traditional vintage performer.

The Caterham Seven first appeared in 1957 as the product of Lotus, and was the work of

Colin Chapman, the man behind many of the most important design advances in later Grand Prix and road car designs. It was a surprisingly dated design even then, but its lightweight virtues have stood spirited motorsport use, and the clichés of many a road-test report, and a new Kentish factory was acquired in late 1987 to help meet steadily increasing international demand.

What are the attributes of this great British survivor? Stunning acceleration, joyful handling and supremely confident cornering are characteristics that any Seven driver will report. Below 100 mph (160 kph), straightline speed is in the exotic car class, but pre-war aerodynamics keep top speed below 120 mph (192 kph).

As in any good design, simplicity has allowed a strong original theme to change subtly with the times. At first sight you would say the Seven has not altered much over the years, yet its simple tubular chassis has accommodated a bewildering variety of standard and modified four-cylinder power units. In the models of the eighties, the chassis tubes, beneath primarily aluminium panelling (the nose cones and wings are of glassfibre), have been repositioned to provide extra leg room and a de Dion rear

suspension arrangement has replaced the old live axle.

Engines have ranged from 48 to 170 bhp in production, and have been mated to an equally broad cross-section of three-, four- and five-speed gearboxes. Similarly, a number of Ford and British Leyland sources provided the live back axles that were employed prior to the 1985 de Dion.

Lotus has always set as fast a pace among road-car designs as it has on the track, so it is really quite

Above Despite such vital additions as alloy wheels and larger, grippier, tyres the Caterham Seven, here in Super Sprint form, is still recognizable as the car Colin Chapman penned so long ago

surprising that it kept the Seven in intermittent production from 1957 to 1973, before handing over manufacturing and sales rights to Caterham Cars in Surrey.

The Seven that Lotus was making at the hand-over point was the glassfibre 'bath tub' S4 model, but that proved an impractical production proposition for an outside concern and it had never been accepted as a 'real' Seven. In September 1974 Caterham resumed production of

. . . the Super Sprint, even at close to 1200 lb (545 kg), is in a different class; just over 110 mph and a Ferrari/Porsche baiting 5.6 seconds to 60 mph . . .

the classic alloy-panel S3, in Twin Cam power trim, and has continued subtle development ever since.

But the essential elements remain – a stylish low-weight soft-top, equipped with front-

of power specifications, from the basic 'production' single-carburettor 84 bhp to the Sprint (110 bhp) and Super Sprint (135 bhp).

Even equipped with just that 84 bhp, 0-60 mph (96 kph), with that 1100 lb (500 kg) kerb weight, can be accomplished in 7.7 seconds, but top speed is lower than that of many family saloons, at some 100 mph (160 kph). The Sprint power level clips tenths off the acceleration time and pushes the car closer to the 110 mph (176 kph) mark, but the Super Sprint, even at close to 1200 lb

mounted engine driving the rear wheels. Even during Caterham's custody, engine specifications have varied dramatically. As for the rest of the car, much of the initial 'development' comprised simply finding new sources of supply, and this applied particularly to the original Lotus Twin Cam.

Several alternative power units were tested, from a Garrett turbocharged engine to Vegantune's own twin cam. Yet the backbone of Seven horsepower has always been the simple Ford Kent crossflow, an engine that first became familiar to British motorists in the 1960s through the second generation of Cortinas.

Today, continuity of supply of these pushrod power units is assured by Ford, which has to meet the demand of Formula Ford and industrial users. The plain four-cylinder engine can be supplied by Caterham in a variety

Left In Super Sprint 1.7-litre pushrod form, the Caterham Seven's Ford engine pumps out an impressive 135 bhp – enough to produce a 5.6 secs 0-60 time

Below Making the most of a spartan interior with red leather for the steering wheel and trim

(545 kg) kerb weight, is in a different class altogether: just over 110 mph (176 kph) and a Ferrari/Porsche-bating 5.6 seconds to 60 mph (96 kph), according to *Autocar*. Expect less than 25 mpg from the most powerful derivative, but the standard 84 bhp will manage 27-30 mpg.

Some people, notably the Japanese, are not satisfied with the sort of acceleration rates provided by modified pushrod engines. At first, Caterham met such demand by using the Twin Cam Lotus motor, but when that engine was discontinued, the company replaced it with the Cosworth-Ford-sourced four-cylinder BDR. This is another twin-overhead-camshaft design, but has four valves per cylinder and the choice of 155 bhp (1.6) or a whopping 170 bhp (1.7).

Such power – the 1200 lb (545 kg) machine will reach 120 mph (192 kph) and blasts from standstill to 60 mph (96 kph) in exactly 5 seconds – is only sold in association with an advanced driving course. Nothing outside the Lamborghini V12 category can match such acceleration.

Although the braking components are far from specialized, the Seven's low weight contributes to stopping abilities that match the overwhelming acceleration. Big improvements have been made over the first Sevens in terms of ride quality, cockpit comfort and bumpy road stability as well as performance. However, the car remains noisy and draughty by contemporary standards.

The ethos of the Seven in 1988 is as when the late Colin Chapman conceived it: so much affordable fun that you care only about the car's charismatic strong points and are able to overlook the inevitable snags of such an uncompromising and durable concept. Long may it continue. . . .

CORVETTE
CHEVROLET

Conceived in 1951 as a low-cost fun car, Chevrolet's Corvette went into limited production in 1953 and has survived as America's only mass-produced sports car today. The modern 150 mph

Corvette has proved an exciting leader in style as well as in competition; it is also something of a bargain at an American price equivalent to £19 000 (on a depressed US dollar rate) but no 1988 list price was quoted in Britain for the left-hand-drive-only machine.

Despite the perennial rumours of 'a mid-engine 'Vette,' the 1988 production cars cling to principles established in the car's fifties debut: front engine, rear drive and a shapely two-door body in glassfibre.

During its long production run the Corvette has featured six- and eight-cylinder engines in an enormous variety of power outputs and four sharply distinctive

equipped with standard sunroof, and the convertible that arrived in 1986.

Underneath the injection-moulded glassfibre panels of the 0.32 drag coefficient coupé and less aerodynamically qualified convertible, lies a steel frame and uniquely independent suspension, employing alloy wishbones and transverse leaf springs in glassfibre. Recent Corvettes have run exceptionally large wheels and

styles. By 1988, power, from a fuel-injected V8 of 5.7 litres, was heading back upwards, beyond 240 bhp.

Corvette horsepower in the eighties still has a long way to travel to match the gross outputs claimed from the 1969 ZL-1 aluminium V8 option, rated at 585 bhp, or the V8 of 7.4 litres in pre-emission control 1970. Then the company talked of 465 bhp to special order and more than 400 bhp was regularly sold from 1965 onwards via a 6.4-litre V8 – quite a contrast to the 1953 six, its triple carburettors supporting a claim of 150 bhp. . . .

Chevrolet, the biggest mass-production arm of the world's biggest corporation, General Motors, keeps threatening to produce ever more high-tech versions of the Corvette: four-wheel drive, optional four-wheel steering and a mid-engined layout are the most popular rumours. For the moment, however, GM continues to rely on the coupé body style premiered in 1983,

The car rumbles from 0 to 60 mph in 5.3 seconds, clips the standing quarter-mile in 14.2 secs – reaching nearly 100 mph – and has achieved an independently timed 154 mph

255/50VR Goodyear Eagle tyres to generate exceptional cornering forces.

Unfortunately, public roads are not all surfaced with ripple-free tarmacadam, and the American

Far left Chevrolet have spared no effort to make the interior of the current 'Vette as luxurious as possible with almost infinitely power adjustable leather covered seats

Above One of the most impressive electronic dashboard displays in production, with the minor gauges able to display a range of information at the touch of a button

Left Distinctive, and taller, alloy wheels denote the '88 model

Right The looks will not give the game away but this is a Callaway Twin Turbo, a Chevrolet-approved conversion capable of more than 180 mph from its 383 bhp

Below Massive Goodyear 'Gatorbacks' share the under bonnet space of the standard car with a 5.7-litre producing 'only' 243 bhp

public complained vociferously about the car's harsh ride. This was subsequently made more civilized by the adoption of Delco-Bilstein gas-damping and the relegation of some suspension parts to a racing-biased option list.

The Corvette has often premiered features new to the American public, although a number of suppliers on the current models will be familiar to Europeans. For instance, Robert Bosch has cooperated with General Motors in the supply of electronic fuel-injection components, while British Girling

patents are to be found in the four-wheel ventilated-disc braking system.

The Corvette of 1983 also explored some new interior features, particularly the digital dashboard display. Unlike many cursed electronic instrumentation arrays in Europe, GM's information centre was large enough for legibility and made use of graphics, such as the power curve simulation in the tachometer scale, to ensure fast comprehension. Other information that is graphically represented includes oil pressure, water temperature

and battery voltage, but you have the option of deleting subsidiary information to concentrate on speed and rpm. Even on a sunny day at Riverside Raceway in California the big digital speedo could clearly be read beyond 130 mph. . . .

The interior, in European style, avoids excess. A plain two-spoke steering wheel complements bucket seating that can comfortably accommodate a Texan. Plastics within are generally of high grade, and garish colour combinations are avoided.

Standard equipment varies according to model year, but more than ninety per cent of Corvettes are sold equipped with automatic transmission. This is basically a three-speed unit with a fuel economy overdrive available; the four-speed manual also has an electronically activated overdrive.

A limited-slip differential is standard, and all Corvettes in recent years have tended to run exceptionally 'tall' final drive ratios, meaning their large V8 engines rumble along at fuel-consciously low rpm when cruising at the American 55–65 mph (88–104 kph) speed limits. Even at 150 mph (240 kph) the 5733 cc unit turns at under 4200 rpm.

Also on the standard equipment list are giant alloy wheels (9.5 x 16 inch), central locking, electronic windows, tinted glass, anti-lock braking and GM's unique Delco steering rake/reach adjustment. That can be combined with power seats to make a stranger to the car quickly comfortable. Air conditioning is among the most popular options, along with a

wide variety of in-car stereo equipment.

The 1987 model Corvette has a rather ponderous manual gearbox hitched to a V8 of 243 bhp at a lazy 4000 revs. This gentle giant runs a 9.4:1 compression ratio in its alloy cylinder heads, with the camshaft located in the iron block of the 90-degree vee. At 3200 rpm, 345 lb ft of torque is generated.

The car rumbles from 0 to 60 mph in 5.3 seconds, clips the standing quarter-mile in 14.2 secs – reaching nearly 100 mph – and has achieved an independently timed 154 mph. You could expect 17–20 mpg in European use, but gentler cruising in America would return slightly over 20 British mpg.

For those who want to go faster still, Callaway in Connecticut, USA, executes a warranted twin turbocharger conversion that yields 383 bhp and a staggering 545 lb ft of torque. This docile and highly mobile power station is capable of more than 180 mph, and sprints from 0 to 60 mph in 4.5 secs, while an aerodynamically modified version was timed at 195.5 mph. The Callaway twin turbo cars cost an additional £14 500 and while the standard car is fast the twin-turbo option brings the Corvette into the more powerful Ferrari, Porsche and Lamborghini class.

Whatever the model, the Corvette's drawling power and considerable cornering capability make it an exciting drive for a European. Efficient supplementary features and unusual chassis engineering have set new standards for front-engined sports car motoring.

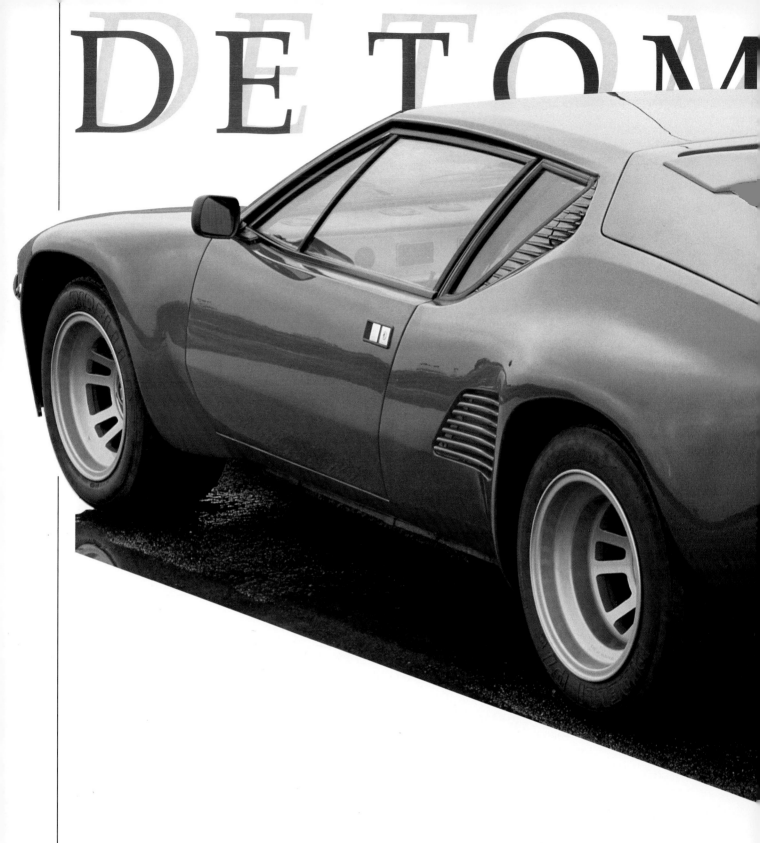

PANTERA GT5-S

DE TOMASO

Born into an era when the combination of cheaply available American V8 horsepower and Italian style was irresistible, the De Tomaso Pantera (Panther) is the longest-lived supercar available outside the replica GT40s and their like. The model

examined here costs £47 621 in 1988, but customers could specify so many details that an unusually wide price spectrum (starting at less than £34 000) applied in Britain.

Originally, Ford thought Americans would be queuing up to buy this exotic cocktail. And it is easy enough to see the logic, since the Cobra and GT40 had brought new respect for the alliance of American brawn and European chassis. However, the Modena-manufactured De Tomaso never has attained the status of these Anglo-American alliances.

The car looks exactly as you would expect of an Italian mid-engined design, but it is executed in steel rather than aluminium, so that its eight-cylinder bulk tips the scale about as much as does Lamborghini's V12 Countach: 3220 lb (1460 kg). Other dimensions are broadly comparable with those of the

Lambo too: it is 168.1 inches (427 cm) long, 77.5 inches (197 cm) wide and less than 43.5 inches (109 cm) high. However, the wheelbase is longer than that of the V12 supercar, measuring 99 inches (251 cm).

The GT5-S specification is given away by the optional large rear wing. There is little chance of mistaking the De Tomaso for anything other than an outright performance machine, since the extended bodywork and deep front spoiler sweep around to

Right The unmistakable rear wing shows that this is a GT5-S spec Pantera

embrace 10- and 13-inch-wide alloy wheels. Their 15-inch circumferences are clothed by Pirelli P7s, a fat 285/40 for the steered front wheels and 345/35 for the back.

The dramatic exterior is accompanied by a plush, sporting cabin. The trim on the large central console matches the leather-clad seats and the five-speed gearbox, with its shiny gate, has a racing feel to it.

Besides the paired tachometer and speedometer, a quartet of auxiliary dials is arranged vertically alongside the upturned radio/cassette, but beneath the standard air-conditioning controls. These monitor oil pressure, water temperature, charge current and the content of the 17.5-gallon (80-litre) fuel tank.

The running gear surrounding that leathery cockpit is also reminiscent of past racing practice. Double-wishbone suspension is offered front and rear, using combined coil spring/telescopic damper units. Front and rear anti-roll bars are fitted, the back anti-roll bar coiling around the rearmost section of the lengthy transaxle and the engine is placed well forward of the axle line, in a truly

There is little chance of mistaking the De Tomaso for anything other than an outright performance machine, since the extended bodywork and deep front spoiler sweeps around . . .

mid-engined layout. Despite the central disposition of the engine, weight is biased toward the rear – more than fifty-seven per cent is over the back wheels.

The lighter front end is guided by a three-spoke wheel that actuates unassisted rack-and-pinion steering. Servo-assistance lightens the pedal pressure for the dual-circuit brakes, which comprise 11.2-inch (284 mm) ventilated front discs and larger rear units, of 11.7 inches (297 mm).

De Tomaso and its Silverstone-based British representative Emilia Concessionaires, offer a choice of power outputs ranging from 270 to 350 bhp, and further increases are available on request. Power is supplied by Ford's family of 90-degree, cast-iron V8s; by the late 1980s De Tomaso had centred upon the Cleveland Fords – 5.7-litre units that have also propelled Thunderbirds and Mustangs, AC Cobras and GT40s.

The GT5-S sampled in Britain had been fitted with one of the tuned V8s giving 'well over' 300 bhp. That meant an extremely high compression ratio (10.5:1) and a very large American Holley carburettor containing four chokes. The Cleveland series from Ford normally has hydraulic valve actuation, but for the higher states of tune De Tomaso offers mechanical lifters and a replacement camshaft which together allow the bellowing V8 to reach 7000 lusty rpm.

Burdened by 1.5 tons, one

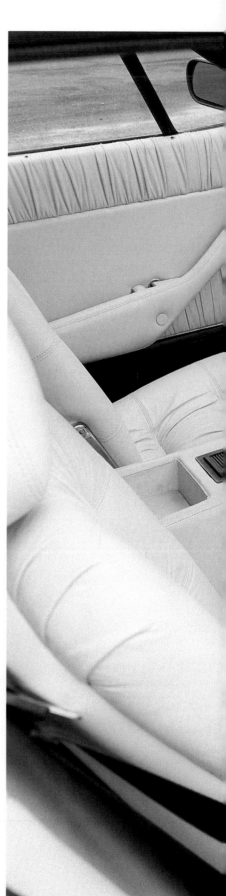

Left Italian supercars have endearing features, like the afterthought of this tacked on reflector . . .

Below It takes a large wheel to hold the Pirelli P7s of 345/35 section used at the rear of the Pantera

Right Just room for two in a surprisingly cramped cabin – again in true supercar tradition

might expect a simple V8 to lose its edge, but the De Tomaso is a rowdily rapid machine. An exceptionally long first gear allows 60 mph (96 kph), if all the available revs of the tuned engine are exploited.

That first gear capability means that a standing-start to the much-quoted mile-a-minute occupies under 5.5 seconds and 0-100 mph (160 kph) takes fractionally over 13 seconds. By that time it has covered a standing quarter-mile, crossing the line at more than 100 mph (160 kph), and is on the way to a maximum which is beyond 160 mph (256 kph). The penalty is a consumption figure of 16-18 mpg during hard use. . . .

The higher-powered V8 delivers the performance of a Porsche 911 Turbo, but in a totally different manner. Whereas the Porsche is a civilized coupé, whose rear-mounted, flat-six engine has a modest, whistling note, the tuned V8 is raucous. The De Tomaso's enormous tyres have terrific adhesion in the dry, but in the wet, it is difficult to drive the Italian car with sufficient delicacy to retain consistent contact with the ground

At parking speeds, one is especially conscious that De Tomaso has provided some of the biggest wheels and tyres ever seen on a road car. The unassisted steering fights the fat treads, while the driver cranes round over his shoulder, peering past the optional wing, or squints into the mirrors, hoping, rather optimistically, for a glimpse of kerb beyond the massive wheel arches.

Left The Pantera's lines shout aggression, something which is provided by over 300 bhp of tuned Ford Cleveland V8 mounted admidships (**right**)

City manoeuvres are further obstructed by a turning circle of close to 40 ft (12·2 metres), but most owners would argue that such a car is purchased for the pursuit of pleasure beyond city limits.

At higher speeds the steering becomes an ally, feeding plenty of information back to the driver, who will no longer be cursing the absence of power assistance. At high or low speed the mid-engined layout and sheer acreage of tyre tread ensure enormous adhesion, and the brakes are capable of generating more than 0.9 g of deceleration.

The De Tomaso Pantera offers cut-price motoring in the 160 mph (256 kph) class. The drawback is that obtaining such performance involves considerable modification to the normally docile and durable V8. The Pantera's survival over the years shows that there are customers who appreciate its individual qualities sufficiently to overlook such snags.

EVANTE

EVANTE

Although Britain in the 1950s and early '60s had a reputation for being the home of the small sports car, many of the cars available were rather crude. They offered sporting performance and open-air motoring, but they could never

have been described as anything other than rudimentary in their chassis design. On the race tracks of the late 1950s, however, things were a little different, and most of this was due to one man. Colin Chapman of Lotus not only produced small racers bearing his own name, but worked on the famous Grand Prix Vanwall and turned that sow's ear into a real silk purse.

His race-chassis mastery was put to good use in the road-going Lotus 7, which remains to this day one of the sharpest-handling road cars available, and he then went on to produce the glassfibre-monocoque Elite which was the first Lotus available with any semblance of luxury and comfort.

Unfortunately, the Elite was very expensive to manufacture, was not the most reliable of cars and suffered because there just weren't enough people who could both afford it and appreciate

its perfect road manners. The opportunity for the public at large to sample a more reasonably priced road-going car with racer manners, wearing the famous yellow-and-green 'ACBC' badge of the founder came at the London Motor Show in 1962. The event, which also saw the arrival of the Triumph Spitfire and the MGB, saw the birth of the Lotus Elan, a car similar in size to the little Triumph, but as roomy as the bigger MG. The Lotus was several classes above both in its dynamic abilities and it became almost a cliché for magazines to mention that it 'set new standards in handling and roadholding'.

Over the next eleven years, the Elan steadily grew in performance as more power was extracted from its twin-cam-headed, Ford-based motor; it got a little more luxurious, but its illustrious

progenitor was careful not to add any bulk to it which would detract from what it did best – run rings around the opposition.

It was in 1973 that the last Elan left the Lotus factory in Wymondham, Norfolk, by which time it had a top speed of around 125 mph, was able to accelerate to 60 mph (96 kph) in under 7 seconds, yet still return over 30 mpg when necessary, courtesy of its efficient 1558 cc, 126 bhp

engine. After '73, Lotus decided to go up-market to chase Porsche sales, and Elans have since become extremely collectable, especially as no other manufacturer since has managed to produce a car which has even come close to matching the *petite* Lotus's capabilities.

Vegantune, of Spalding in the flat fenlands of Lincolnshire, have for many years been Lotus specialists, restoring Elans and

Europas and extracting even more power from their already highly tuned engines. Company boss George Robinson has worked closely with the Lotus factory and has spent a good deal of time discussing his Evante project with them.

George saw the market for used Elans booming and reasoned that there would still be a place for a car like the small Lotus; not just a replica but instead one brought up to date. With this in mind, he started work on the Evante. Lotus are very careful about others copying their parts and cars, so the Evante, although looking for all the world like an Elan, is actually subtly different in every line.

Like the Elan, the Evante is based on a backbone frame featuring a Y-fork at the front, in which the engine sits, and a T-bar at the rear, to which the suspension is attached. However, the chassis of the Spalding car is

Far left The luxury of leather trim and a veneered dashboard are complemented by electric windows – a far cry from the stark nature of early British sports cars

Left 'Vegantune' on the cam covers shows this is no Lotus twin-cam but Vegantune's own 1699 cc 140 bhp, unit

Below left The Evante may look like a Lotus Elan but the lines have been varied in subtle fashion

made from tubular steel rather than steel sheet and it features twin-wishbone suspension at both ends rather than the Lotus rear strut of the Elan. Because of the design of the suspension and the bodywork, the Evante can take 195-section, low-profile tyres, while the Elan had to make do with much narrower wear, and this more than anything brings the Evante up to date. There are Girling discs at each corner to stop it, but it is what makes the Evante go that separates this from many other specialist British sports cars. While other small manufacturers are content to use engines from other manufacturers parts bins, engine specialist George Robinson builds his own motors in much the same way as did Chapman – using a Ford cylinder block. In this case, the VTA

motor has a light-alloy head and a capacity of 1699 cc which, when breathing through two 40 mm twin-choke carburettors, gives the motor 140 bhp and 129 lb ft of torque. George has experimented with four valves per cylinder, but prefers the better low-speed torque of his two-valve VTA – at least until his new and highly innovative four-valve engine is developed. In the meantime, if you need more power, you can opt for a 200 bhp turbocharged motor.

There is a limit to the power that a lightweight sportster can usefully handle: with its glassfibre body, incorporating carbon-fibre and Kevlar strengthening, the Evante weighs a paltry 14.5 cwt (738 kg), which gives the standard 1700 cc car a top speed of just under 140 mph (224 kph), in the uppermost of its five Ford Sierra gears, and acceleration from 0-60 mph (96 kph) in around six seconds.

D989 LCE

That light weight, coupled with a race-bred chassis, makes for brilliant handling and roadholding, as well. With light yet positive steering, the Evante is really at home on twisty byways, its diminutive size allowing rapid progress through tight corners. That combined with the extra grip afforded by the latest low-profile tyres makes for as rapid a machine as you could wish for across country.

The Evante doesn't miss out on the luxury side, either. There is thick carpet in the deep footwells, a luxurious wood-veneered dashboard and electric windows. However, the whole window frame retracts into the doors on the Evante to provide full open-air motoring; something the last electric-windowed Elans couldn't offer.

At over £12 000 in basic form,

Right The Evante's alloy wheels fill the very limits of the arches, showing how much wider rubber it wears than the Elan

Far right All the instrumentation a keen driver could require; the steering column stalk is from the current Ford Escort

Below The flipped-up rear boot line destroys the Elan illusion

plus taxes and delivery, the Vegantune Evante is not cheap, but then again the best Lotus Elans are commanding prices that are scraping into the five-figure bracket. What George Robinson and his team up in Spalding have done is to produce a car which has taken the basic Colin Chapman concept and improved upon it. With over a quarter of a century having passed since the first Elan was produced, that is not surprising. What is more so is that nobody else, big or small, has managed to do that with a small drophead luxury sports car – or will the new Elan for the 1990s from the Lotus factory do that? It will have to be brilliant to be as good as the old Elan and the Evante!

F40

FERRARI

While Porsche made its 200 mph 959 a triumph of high technology, Ferrari went for a simpler approach when building its similarly speedy F40. Instead of all-wheel-drive, six gears and sophisticated electronics, Ferrari chose the 'stripped street racer' philosophy. From towering

rear spoiler to a cabin wearing three drilled pedals, and wrap-around racing seats, the 174.4-inch (4429 mm) red projectile states flatly, 'I am the king of the performance pack'. The maximum speed quoted is the highest for any 'production' car, at slightly in excess of 200 mph (322 kph).

Independent testers had not had the chance to verify Ferrari's claims when this was written, but maximum speed is officially quoted at 324 kph or 201.3 mph in the seductive brochure that was issued to potential purchasers of the £140 000-plus F40. The price depends on whether you are an established Ferrari customer (such as a Testarossa owner trading up),

or a buyer transgressing Ferrari's wishes and paying extra to take over an established order, in which case prices beyond £200 000 were frequently quoted prior to the Stock Exchange crash of late 1987.

Ferrari doesn't bother to discuss acceleration to such a mundane pace as 60 mph (96 kph), the only brochure figures for acceleration

. . . fuel injection manifolding
is fed by twin Behr-labelled
intercoolers and the mighty
turbochargers lurk amongst shiny
exhaust plumbing

being 0-200 kph (124 mph) in 12 seconds. Also, the car covers a standing kilometre (0.621 of a mile) in 21 seconds, the terminal speed being 270 kph (168 mph).

The Porsche 959 tested by Germany's monthly magazine *auto motor und sport* in 1987 produced a maximum of 197 mph (317 kph) in its unique production sixth gear and covered the equivalent of 0-124 mph in 13.3 seconds; 0-62 mph occupied a scant 3.7 seconds. Nevertheless, the Ferrari should be even faster, for the Porsche weighed over 3300 lb (1500 kg) in test trim.

Ferrari announced the F40 at an international press conference in the autumn of 1987, and planned to build at least 400, commencing production in January 1988. The 'F40' tag refers to the fortieth anniversary of the successful Ferrari's first appearance in sports

Left *The interior demonstrates that this Ferrari was built with performance in mind; the cabin is sparse*

Middle & far left *The F40 is built low and squat, again with performance in mind, performance that sees the red missile reach 62 mph (100 kph) in a mere 3.7 seconds*

car racing (March 1947).

The suspension system is special, but not of the ground-effect sports-racing era suggested by the F40's appearance. It comprises a double-wishbone system in 'special-grade tubular steel', but the rear struts used would be more in keeping in a rather more mundane road car.

Dampers, wheels and tyres are suitably specialized, the damping provided by Ferrari's Grand Prix supplier Koni of Holland. The fattest tyres we have seen on a road car – 335/35 section at the rear – are mounted on shimmering five-spoke Speedline wheels. These measure 17 inches in diameter, and are 8 inches broad at the front, 13 inches at the back – this Ferrari rolls along on Pirelli P Zero rubber that is more than twice the width of that on some sports saloons.

Throughout the F40 there are few concessions to customer comfort. Neither the rack-and-pinion steering, nor the enormous ventilated disc brakes (13-inch diameter) have power-assistance. Skilled drivers usually regard such assisted systems as unnecessary

luxuries that spoil the feel to be had through palms and feet. Most racing formula cars lack power-assistance, so the lack of vacuum, hydraulic or electronic devices is in keeping with Ferrari F40 philosophy.

The cockpit, sporting racing red seats and Sabelt full harness, underlines the 'road racer' image, as do the Momo three-spoke steering wheel and dials for revs, speed, turbocharger boost, water and oil temperatures, oil pressure and fuel contents in the twin tanks that together accommodate 26.4 gallons (120 litres).

Air-conditioning is optional, but there is no obvious place to fit a radio, which might be regarded as a frivolous distraction in such a car. Gridded and drilled pedals add just a little more to the macho racing character of the car, as does the wide use of perspex for the side and rear windows. The untrimmed side doors have panes that slide back and forth in a frame, rather than wind-down windows.

Judging by the strong demand from the world's millionaires, Ferrari has hit just the right note by producing a road car which reminds its customers so vividly of the company's reason for existence: motor racing.

However, the F40 shares neither Ferrari's flat-twelve nor its V12 design, relying on twin turbochargers to extract an awesome 478 bhp from its aluminium V8. This unit is an enlarged development of the 2855 cc V8 that powered Ferrari's earlier limited-production exoticar, the 288 GTO.

Mounted beneath the vented rear screen of its slippery (0.34 Cd) body, the F40's 2936 cc V8 incorporates every high-performance aid to provide the world's most powerful production engine. A pair of Japanese IHI turbochargers runs at 1.1 bar/15.7 psi and feeds cylinder heads containing thirty-two valves and double overhead camshafts on each of the 90-degree cylinder banks.

Managed by Weber-Marelli electronic injection and ignition systems, this astounding power unit is rated for safe operation to 7750 rpm and provides more than 425 lb ft of torque. With a weight of only 2420 lb (1100 kg) the only road car with which the Ferrari's performance can be compared is Porsche's 959, or one of the smaller C2 sports cars that this fiery Ferrari echoes in so many ways.

Looking around this magnificent motor car, the most impressive feature is its striking appearance, and the quality of the

Right
Overshadowed by two huge intercoolers, the engine is not the flat- or V12 you might expect but a V8, albeit one that produces 478 bhp at 7000 rpm thanks to those two IHI turbos

Below Built to commemorate 40 years of Ferrari cars the F40 is, according to Ferrari '... a definite product of the racing cars and represents the technical synthesis of intensive research'

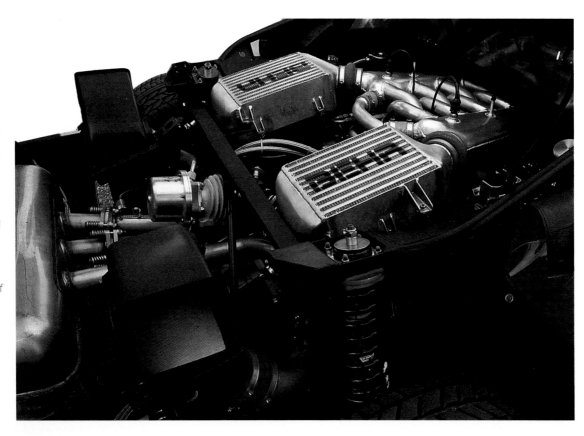

varied metallic castings. Another highlight is the engine bay, where fuel-injection inlet manifolding is fed by twin Behr-labelled intercoolers and the mighty power plant's turbochargers, lurk amongst shiny exhaust plumbing. A pair of oval exhausts sandwiches the wastegate vent, protuberant beneath the rear tail-light panel. The triple pipes sprout in the central 'island' amongst emerging 'ground-effect tunnels' – a reminder of its racing heritage.

Seen at motor shows, the F40 crams plenty of such reminders into its 78 inches (1981 mm) width and lowline 44.5-inch (1130 mm) height. Chief of these is the strategic use of composite Kevlar and carbon fibres to reinforce the body and clothe the steel-alloys that comprise the basic tubular construction.

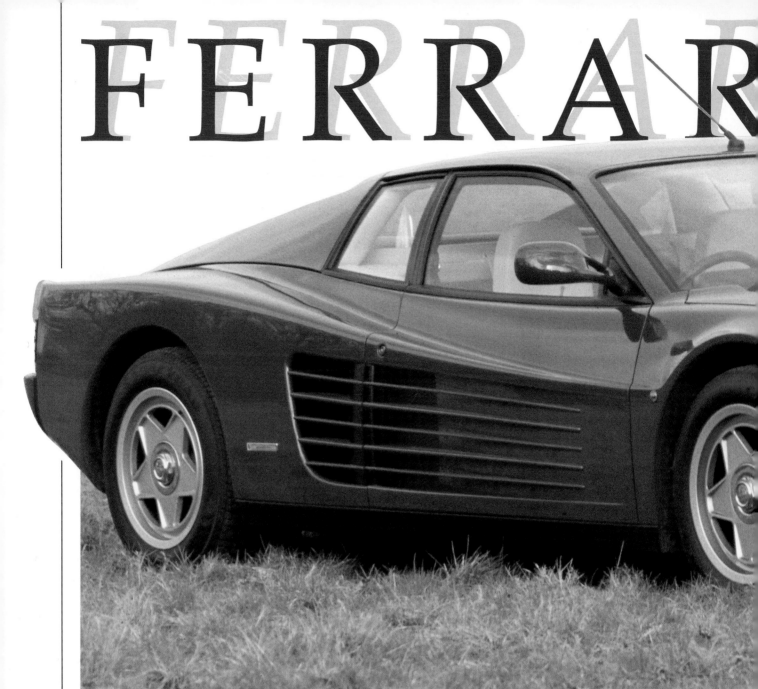

TESTAROSSA
FERRARI

All Ferraris have glamour, but the sight of a new Testarossa (it means 'redhead' and recalls a 1956 Ferrari sports racer) will turn heads anywhere, anytime. If the standard Pininfarina coupé is not sufficient, then Richard Straman in the USA will transform it into a full convertible,

E272 DPK

or build a targa top. The cachet of the Testarossa is not just its 180 mph (280 kph) top speed, but the sheer physical presence of this side-slatted beauty.

Almost everything about the Testarossa is on a grand scale, the major exception being the cockpit ahead of the mid-mounted engine – a cabin which caters only for a twosome and their squashiest luggage. More luggage space is provided beneath the raked bonnet and its concealed headlamps. The rear decklid reveals a seductively presented twelve-cylinder powerhouse. From the curving silver induction tubes of its Bosch K-Jetronic fuel injection, to the red finish of the rocker covers that gave the car the testarossa name, this Ferrari flat-twelve represents mechanical art at its best.

Arranged longitudinally above a five-speed transmission, this majestic engine translates into production form the heritage of Ferrari's 3-litre flat-twelve racing engines – World Championship

Left Under the massive induction system can be seen the red cam covers that give this Ferrari its *testarossa* (red head) name

Right The distinctive side stracks partly conceal the side-mounted radiators

winners in sports and Grand Prix racing. A closer mechanical relative was the Ferrari Berlinetta Boxer (BB 512i), which the Testarossa replaced shortly after its public debut at the Paris International Motor Show of autumn 1984.

With the exception of turbocharging, the Testarossa features every performance

feature that a British customer would expect when paying more than £86 701 for a car. Displacing 4942 cc in two six-cylinder banks, each topped by four valves per cylinder and double overhead camshafts, this engine is pretty spectacular.

Instead of concentrating on ultimate power, the Maranello engineers worked upon the provision of supreme flexibility. Thus the peak output of 390 bhp at 6300 rpm is accompanied by 362 lb ft of meaty torque to pull the 3311 lb (1505 kg) body along at enormous speeds.

Revved to the safe maximum of 6800 rpm in the lower ratios, the Testarossa pounces from rest to 62 mph in 5.8 secs, disposing of the quarter-mile in 13.6 seconds. Only one kilometre was needed to reach 144 mph (231 kph). The German magazine *auto motor und sport* verified a maximum of 291 kph, equivalent to 180.7 mph. The penalty for such weighty speed, however, is an overall

15.3 mpg. The German price quoted for the car was considerably less than that in England: translated from Deutschmarks at the prevailing 3DM to every £ it was equivalent to £77 766.

Pininfarina has been associated with all the most beautiful Ferraris, and the Testarossa, one of the biggest Ferraris yet, is no exception. Constructed over a tubular chassis frame whose rear section detaches to afford access to engine and transmission, Pininfarina's body extends to 176.6 inches (4485 mm).

The width at 77.8 inches (1976 mm) is in the competition car class, while the height fits in with the low-slung appearance at just over 44 inches (1130 mm). Incidentally, the side slats are necessary since the engine is cooled via 1970s-racing-style side radiators.

The running gear to complement the prestigious power unit is slightly unusual in

Right The ribbed side treatment is continued around to the rear across the lights. The low, wide look is no illusion – the Testarossa is some 77.8 inches wide

Far right Another of the Testarossa's immediately recognizable features is the door mirror on its long stalks

providing two dampers and attendant coil springs for each of the box-section rear wishbone pairs. Front suspension is more conventional, using triangulated double wishbones and a single coil spring/shock absorber unit for each corner.

Anti-roll bars are fitted front and rear, and tyres are either Goodyears or Michelin's unique TRX series. In the case of the former, sizes are 255/50VR-16, on 10-inch-wide rims at the back and 225/50VR-16, with 8-inch rims, at the front.

To halt such an imposing two-seater, Ferrari specifies some of the biggest ventilated disc brakes seen on a road car. Servo-assisted and drawing further support from a hydraulic pump, they measure 12.2 inches (310 mm) at the rear and fractionally less at the front.

Unlike the enormous disc brakes, the rack-and-pinion steering has no power assistance. Since its turning circle is close to 40 ft the Testarossa is not the most agile choice for city streets, particularly in view of the inevitably restricted rearward vision, which is not helped by the fact that only one elegant door frame mirror is standard.

Matching the supercar's performance – you can hang on to fourth gear beyond 130 mph before a change into fifth is needed – is the adhesive chassis

The interior is simple in comparison to those of many less-prestigious performance cars. There is a large three-spoke steering wheel, trimmed in black leather and bearing the Prancing Horse emblem.

Ahead of the driver, the colour of the plastic fascia trim does not necessarily match the shade of leather used to trim seats and much of the surroundings, but the carpeting does accord with the high-grade plastics.

Instrumentation is not as complex as many other aircraft-styled displays described in this

The Testarossa's interior is remarkably unassuming but has particularly nice features such as the Ferrari prancing horse moulded on the bonnet catch next to the hand brake

hinged lid that folds down over the radio to hide it away.

The controls, though hardly complex, are mostly obedient and although the gear change is not the fastest in the world, so many Ferrari litres are at your disposal that it doesn't matter – any pressure on the accelerator in top gear swiftly builds both joyful exhaust note and smoothly attained speed.

Matching this supercar's performance – you can hang on to fourth gear beyond 130 mph (208 kph) before a change into fifth is needed – is the adhesive and good-natured chassis. Cornering ability is best summarized by America's *Road & Track*, which said, 'It's a marvellously neutral handling car that tracks around the curves with Velcro-like security'.

book, but the orange-numbered dials are certainly large enough to command attention, particularly the 10 000 rpm tachometer (red-lined from 6800 onward) and the right-hand-drive model's 200 mph (360 kph) speedometer.

Between the major dials, water temperature and oil temperature are monitored and one neat, if unfortunately necessary, detail is a

FORD

GT40
SAFIR

Once upon a time, the mighty Ford Motor Company decided that it wanted a racing wing, so in 1963 it offered to buy Ferrari. When Enzo said 'no', it was then decided that if the company couldn't join him, it would beat him. Thus, Ford set about building a car to win the prestigious Le

Mans 24-hour race. After much planning, much more work and even more spending, that goal was achieved in 1966 with the MkII and followed in the following year with the awesome, 7-litre MkIV. By that time, the GT40 had already run in both 1964 and '65. Strange then that it wasn't until 1968 that it actually won, and repeated the dose again in '69! It was in that race that the closest ever finish at Le Mans was recorded, with the winning car of Ferrari Grand Prix star Jacky Ickx and Jackie Oliver (now boss of the Arrows Grand Prix team) just managing to stay ahead to beat their Porsche challenger by less than a second!

Although the GT40 was a successful race car, Ford wanted to capitalize on their track success and produce a series of road cars. They had intended to build twenty-five but in the end, JW Automotive (who campaigned the '69 winner and later went on to race Porsches in the same Gulf colours) only

. . . a classic sports car, one which reached the pinnacle of success on the track and which has gone down in motoring legend as one of the greatest successes of all time

completed a handful. These road cars were called GT40 MkIIIs and featured longer tails for luggage, opening side windows, re-sited headlamps, different suspension, a central (rather than right-sill-mounted) gear lever, full trim and chromium over-riders. Today, the road-going GT40s are much prized collector's items.

The GT40 (its name comes from its height, which is actually 40.5 in (102.9 cm)) is back in production – not as a replica but as a continuation of the previous run,

Below Safir's GT40 is a continuation of Ford's own sports racer and matches the original wherever possible.

Right The right-hand-mounted gearlever and the comprehensive display of instruments

and it has the full blessing of JW, who built the originals for Ford, and Ford themselves.

Len Bailey, the famed chassis designer, was product engineer on the original, looking after much of the chassis and suspension design. He has reworked the car to suit road use and the Safir Engineering GT40 MkV has a zinc-coated sheet-steel semi-monocoque chassis, with square-tube stiffening, which is then clad with glassfibre panels. To see a MkV under construction is like looking back twenty years in time to when the originals were emerging from their Slough factory.

The MkVs look very much like racing cars when their bodywork is removed, for there is classic twin-wishbone suspension at the front, coupled with double trailing arms at the rear and massive ventilated 12-inch AP discs at each corner. Just as the early GT40s did, the MkV relies on the classic 289 Ford

V8 engine as the basis of its power unit – the engine which also powered the fabled Ford Mustang and the AC Cobra. By the time the car won Le Mans in '69 it was running 4942 cc and was fitted with Gurney-Weslake heads, but the MkV sticks to the classic 4736 cc capacity.

The engine may be rather antiquated in design, with its single, central camshaft and two pushrod-operated valves per cylinder, but is tuned to produce a whopping 350 bhp at 7500 rpm and 330 lb ft of torque at 5500 rpm. That, in a car weighing just over a ton, means lightning acceleration and an immense top speed. Bear in mind that the 1969 winner had 440 bhp and managed 190 mph (304 kph), and you will understand that the Safir car is plenty quick enough.

The power is taken through an AP twin-plate clutch, which makes town driving rather awkward, and onwards to a ZF five-speed gearbox; on this car the gearchange is where it was

originally intended to be – protruding from the right-hand sill. The rest of the running gear is as original, with gorgeous BRM cast-magnesium six-spoke wheels; however, these are fitted with modern BF Goodrich Comp T/A tyres of 215 section at the front and much wider 255 section at the rear.

In history, there have been just a few cars which have a 'classic' look about them. The GP Bugatti 35 was one, the E-type Jaguar was another and the Ford GT40 is one more. Its combination of shark-like nose, bulbous wings and low, sleek stance make it timeless and its racing success of course enhances that.

The MkV is identical to the Ford, but also harks back to the MkII predecessor of the GT40, in that it

Above The Safir's engine and transaxle take up most of the room under the body-work which hinges back

Far left This particular car has been built with an open roof which makes it much more comfortable to drive around town, although that treatment is flagrant abuse of such a machine!

Left The wheels of the MkV GT40 are made specially for it and match the expensive originals

is available in Spyder form. Instead of the doors being the standard items which curve over at the top and follow the roof line to the centre of the car, the Spyder has short doors and open air where the roof would normally be. This helps, the interior being quite a tight fit – as it in fact needs to be for a race car. The original was built to house no less than 35 gallons (160 litres) of fuel in bag tanks fitted in the sills, but now the present car has to make do with just twin 12-gallon (55-litre) items. Those bulky sills are still there, though, and it means that the two seats (the GT40 was only an 'occasional two-seater', to get around sports-car regulations) are very close together: your passenger had better be a very good friend!

The classic GT40 dashboard is retained, with a speedometer at one end, a tachometer at the other and the minor dials situated in a row in between, and there is also the classic hole-ventilated material covering the seats – essential in a hot cockpit for a 24-hour race.

The Safir GT40 MkV isn't cheap at around £100,000 – really the sky is the limit on price, depending on what specification you choose. The engine, for example, can be tuned up to over 400 bhp and many of the suspension components can be manufactured of lighter material, which will enhance the car's performance even more. If you have the money, Safir, of Brooklands in Surrey, will supply the car to your exact specification.

What you will have is a classic sports car, one which reached the pinnacle of success on the track and which has gone down in motoring legend as one of the greatest successes of all time. 'Your car' will not be a replica, but a continuation of production of the original legend (all those involved with the Ford say so!). It will also have the performance, handling and roadholding of the original, which will make even the most exotic supercars of today seem second-best by comparison.

FORD

RS200

FORD

The Ford reputation rests on producing reliable means of transport rather than turbocharged two-seaters, but every once in a while the company breaks out. The 1987 purchases by Ford of Aston Martin and AC Cars suggest new 1990s life from Ford in the

field of exotica.

Ford's biggest post-war exotic success was the Anglo-American GT40. That 200 mph (322 kph) family of V8 Fords conquered Le Mans three times in the '60s and provided the inspiration for two later two-seaters which attacked rallying under the Ford banner:

the GT70 (abandoned after only half a dozen had been built) and the 1983-6 RS200, which was arguably the most advanced and exciting car sold to the public beneath a Ford badge.

The RS200 was built purely to compete. The 'RS' in its name stood for Rallye Sport (Ford's usual

badge for cars to be used in motorsport) and the '200' signified the number of cars that were to be built. Ford constructed half a dozen prototypes, after the September 1983 managerial approval date, and the remaining 194 were assembled during 1985-6 at the Reliant plant in

Shenstone, Staffs.

The price of the 140 mph (225 kph) RS200 in Britain was £49 950 including taxes. For the forty-eight that were left in 1988 stock, the company raised the price to £52 950, despite the fact that selling a car designed for an obsolescent motorsport formula is a protracted and expensive process. You can reckon that Ford spent over £12 million in manufacturing and designing this RS model, which sadly then had an international competition life of less than one season, owing to a swift change in regulations.

Technically the RS200 is a 157.5-inch (4000 mm) long knock-out from the engineering draughtsmanship of Ford Motorsport's John Wheeler and TWR-Jaguar's 1987 World Sports Car Championship designer, Tony Southgate. The glassfibre body panels clothe a formula car monocoque of aluminium honeycomb, and some body components are locally reinforced in space-age aramid fibres and carbon composites.

Packed into its Ford-Ghia outline, sporting Sierra windscreen and tail-lights, are sophisticated four-wheel-drive (4WD), formula car suspension with twin dampers at each corner, massive ventilated disc brakes front and rear and mid-mounted Ford-Cosworth engine. The four-cylinder unit features intercooled turbocharging, four valves per cylinder and double overhead camshafts.

The RS200s sold to the public (over half were sold outside the UK, at least three to Japan) carry

the clout of 250 horsepower, produced from 1.8 litres and allowing the all-wheel-drive machine to sprint from rest to 60 mph (96 kph) in 6.1 seconds. The maximum speed is 140 mph (225 kph), but the RS200's forte is its rough road speed.

For competition, the works

RS200s had almost doubled horsepower on top: one tested before the 1986 RAC Rally of Great Britain had 450 bhp and could reach 60 mph (96 kph) in 2.8 seconds, about as fast as a Grand Prix racer. The choice of gearing restricted this car to a top speed of 118 mph (190 kph), but it could

The near £50 000 road car rides on generous 8-inch wide alloy wheels that carry a new generation of Pirelli tyres . . . From the driving seat there seems to be almost endless grip . . .

accelerate to 100 mph (161 kph) in 7.3 secs, similar to the time that a quick road car (such as BMW's 325i) takes to reach 60 mph. . . .

The near-£50 000 road cars ride on generous 8-inch-wide alloy wheels that carry what was a new generation of Pirelli tyres, P700s, on the car's announcement. From the driving seat there seems to be almost endless grip, going or slowing, though the restricted view makes parking difficult. The five-speed gearbox is one of the most obstructive ever sold to the public, but the reward is a vehicle with supreme cross-country ability.

For the Ford works team at

Standard Ford components proliferate in the RS200's interior. But why two gear levers? The red one is the real gear lever, the black one the transfer lever – the RS200 was not a permanent four-wheel-drive design remember

Boreham airfield in Essex, the competition career of the RS200 began like a dream. The car not only won its debut race, but also beat, on home ground, its biggest British rival, Austin Rover's Metro 6R4. That was in September 1985; in February 1986 the car undertook its first international. The Swedish rally was an appropriate debut because Ford's drivers were from Sweden, too. Ford team-leader Stig Blomqvist did not finish, but Kalle Grundel slid over icy lakes and tracks to third place.

Unfortunately, this glowing international debut did not preview a more successful future.

Rallying itself was in turmoil after May 1986 because of the deaths of Finland's Henri Toivonen and his co-driver, Sergio Cresto. Ford, particularly, became very apprehensive about safety standards in the sport following two crowd incidents in Ireland and Portugal that involved the RS200. Thus the car did not

Right Glassfibre body panels lift up front and rear to reveal an aluminium honeycomb monocoque combining strength with low weight

Far right Power comes from 1.8 litres of intercooled turbocharged four-cylinder twin-cam. The intercooler is visible at the top of the car with its pipes ducting cold air to the intake

participate in anything like a full programme.

The RS200 did lead a World Championship qualifier, briefly running first and second in Greece, but that Swedish result looked like the highlight of its career when the factory cars were withdrawn at the close of 1986, no longer allowed in world-class competition for 1987. This was not so, however. By then Mark Lovell had won the British home International Rally Championship title in an RS200, and half a dozen of the former rally cars were released to take part in the spectacular TV sport of rallycross.

The rallycross cars are still competing at the time of writing, Britain's 1987 RAC national championship going to northerner Mark Rennison at the wheel of an RS200. Competition development of former factory equipment has resulted in the extraction of more than 620 bhp from the 2.1-litre engines, so the RS200 lives on in the late eighties as a sporting example of how individual a car a large multinational *can* produce.

FORD

SIERRA RS500 COSWORTH

FORD

Another in Ford's limited-edition line of motor sport specials, the Sierra RS500 succeeded the RS200 and was designed for a specific task. That task was to help Ford win the 1987 World Touring Car Championship and in eleven qualifying rounds,

from Britain to New Zealand via Japan and points west, that is exactly what this 'Super Sierra' did.

As in the case of the RS200 the initials and numbers had significance: 'RS' stood for Rallye Sport and '500' denoted the number of cars international regulations demanded should be produced before the car could race. These Sierras were sold during 1987 at a British price of £19 950 and in RHD form only. This was pricey for a Ford, even one timed beyond 145 mph (233 kph), but the company reckoned it could have 'sold another 150, or more', so the car succeeded commercially as well as competitively.

Totally unlike the RS200 the RS500 was a competition special, one based on an existing product: not just any old Sierra GL, but a high-performance model called the Sierra RS Cosworth. Features that lifted this model above the

repmobiles included the Ford Cosworth 204 horsepower engine, an American five-speed gearbox, four-wheel disc braking, with an electronic anti-lock system as standard, and modified suspension.

Externally there was no mistaking an RS for a standard Sierra as every example had an enormous rear wing as part of a body kit that would allow racing teams the best aerodynamics and the widest wheels and tyres.

Built from the humble body of a three-door L, the Sierra RS Cosworth had already established its commercial and competitive worth, the RS500 took things a step further.

For a start, the RS500s had an extensive pedigree. Apart from Ford of Britain's traditional alliance with Northamptonshire's racing engine genius at Cosworth, the RS500 also benefited from hand assembly of all its components at Aston Martin Tickford. If you wanted to stretch a point, and annoy both companies, you could

say this was the first 'Aston Ford', although Tickford, bought by CH Industrials in 1984, had long been financially independent of its founders at Aston Martin.

What made the RS500 faster than the already swift 204 horsepower Sierra RS Cosworth? In a word, 'more' – that is, more of everything that matters in circuit racing: power and roadholding.

Externally the clues were in subtle modifications of the earlier Sierra RS, such as the addition of a small extension 'lip' to the top rear wing, and a secondary spoiler at the back. Together with an extension of the front spoiler, these allowed more wind pressure on the bodywork to push the RS500 into firmer contact with track or road surface. As speed rose and aerodynamic effect was enhanced, so Ford and Cosworth had to ensure that the car was as fast as possible.

The cast-iron, 2-litre cylinder block (which traced its parentage to a simpler 98 bhp 'Pinto' motor found in the old Cortina) was

The highest independently timed speed during the season was 170.8 mph (275 kph) at Bathurst, Australia, but there was little doubt that the Sierras could travel even faster . . .

Above The interior is unpretentious but totally functional

Right The outrageous rear wing is also totally functional

already equipped with every '80s performance aid: intercooled Garrett AiResearch turbocharger, cast-aluminium cylinder head, comparatively high turbo compression ratio of 8:1, four valves per cylinder, double overhead camshafts and electronically managed fuel injection and ignition.

To extract more power from this already potent RS base, Ford and Cosworth engineers enlarged both the turbocharger and its intercooler air radiator. For racing purposes the RS500 also incorporated a secondary rail of fuel injectors. These and sundry other modifications from Swiss specialist Eggenberger (Ford's contracted racing representative in 1986-8) allowed enormous extra horsepower, contained by a stronger cylinder block.

The £19 950 Sierra RS500 sold to the public had 224 bhp instead of the previous RS Sierra's 204. This was enough to reach a claimed 153 road-going mph (246 kph), but that was nothing in comparison to the capabilities of the racing and rally models. For rallying Ford had to use the 'ordinary' RS Cosworth (under a gentlemen's safety agreement, power was limited to 300 bhp), but even that allowed scalding acceleration – 0-60 mph (96 kph), in 5.1 seconds as opposed to the already rapid 6.2 seconds of the production RS.

And the racers were in another class altogether. Even before the RS500 arrived, Ford was reporting that the Eggenberger competition cars were geared to reach over 198.7 mph (320 kph), generated

from a reported 350-385 bhp; the power level could be adjusted from the cockpit via a turbocharger boost control.

When the RS500 arrived Ford had reasons, both political and for safety, for not exaggerating the horsepower achieved, merely quoting 'more than 400 bhp'. In fact, fellow Ford teams with less horsepower reported 480 racing horsepower as routine, and during an annual prize-giving ceremony, rival BMW credited the RS500 with '600 to 650 bhp'. The highest independently timed speed during the season was 170.8 mph (275 kph) at Bathurst, Australia, but there was little doubt that the racing Sierras could travel even faster, given enough space.

The RS500 Sierras were assembled at their British base in the summer of 1987 and granted official racing recognition from

Far left The Pinto-based Cosworth twin-cam is fed by a huge Garrett turbocharger helping it to produce 224 bhp

Left When Ford put the Cosworth Sierra into full production it was in noticeably softened form and in the Sierra Sapphire bodyshell

Below left The unmistakable lines of an instant classic, an immensely rewarding car for those with the skill to exploit its capabilities

1 August of that year. The results were immediate. All season the black and red Texaco-backed works Fords had struggled against BMW's smaller but agile M3 saloons of 285-300 bhp. Now the Fords were in a different class, pulling away to win five of the six remaining World Championship rounds. Prior to the RS500's Czechoslovakian racing debut, Ford had won just one of five World Championship rounds, so the newcomer immediately established the kind of crushing racing superiority that is rarely found.

But what is the RS500 like to drive on the road? The answer is that it has little in common with any other Sierra, save the previous RS. It is not an impractical beast, being perfectly content to idle gently and obediently through city traffic. The controls are far from the heavyweight items featured in many exotic 145 mph (233 kph) sports cars, and power assistance is provided for the steering and the brakes.

It took 1000 rpm more than the previous RS to wake up the bigger turbocharger and release the extra performance potential, but in the 0-60 mph (96 kph) sprint, could be relied upon to skim the 6-second barrier that separates the performers from the poseurs. It will reach at least 145 mph (233 kph) while an mpg figure of 19-21 is quite likely.

The Sierra RS Cosworth Fords, particularly the RS500 with its world-class racing heritage, serve as a reminder that mass-production cars cannot all be dismissed as boring 'Euro-boxes'.

COUNTACH
LAMBORGHINI

I it may be almost unknown on the race track but Lamborghini has become Italy's alternative supercar manufacturer. The only concern consistently to challenge Ferrari for the honour of building the country's fastest production car, Lamborghini has

survived under a number of owners, the latest being Chrysler USA, which acquired the company in 1987.

And since the founder first conferred his name on his brainchild in 1963, it has produced some genuine performance standard-bearers. Equipped with fabulous V8 and V12 motors, they have all been beautiful and fast, from the Espada to the transverse-engined Miura. But none has been faster – independently checked beyond 180 mph (288 kph) – than the extraordinary 455-horsepower Countach 5000S *quattrovalvole*. Its UK list price, at £82 277, is as breathtaking as its power, but there appears to be no shortage of suitably wealthy customers.

Everyone wants to know which is the world's fastest production car. We believe this Lamborghini was certainly the fastest car of its 1985-7 era, and to date it is still one of the fastest machines to be

independently performance-checked.

Ferrari claims its recently launched F40 has the highest maximum speed, at more than 201 mph (322 kph). The fastest car *auto motor und sport* had tested prior to the F40 was the Porsche 959, which it credited with 197 mph (317 kph) on an official 450 bhp.

That magazine also electronically checked the Countach's performance, reporting 0-62 mph (100 kph) in 4.8 seconds and a measured maximum of 186 mph (298 kph).

The German magazine also told its readers that the Ferrari was appreciably slower: 0-62 mph (100 kph) in 5.7 seconds and 181 mph (291 kph) – positively lethargic!

The basic ingredients of the Countach have existed since 1971, when the Bertone two-seater dazzled onlookers at the Geneva Show. Beneath the cowled headlamps and aggressively styled concoction of scoops and spoilers lay the positively vast longitudinally mounted twelve-cylinder engine that ensured no more than strict two-seat

accommodation behind that steeply raked windscreen.

That 1971 Countach continued the company tradition of giving its fastest flagships names that have bull-breeding connections: Lamborghini's emblem is a charging bull, recalling Signore Lamborghini's background in agricultural machinery.

What does 5000S and *quattrovalvole* imply? Simply that Lamborghini likes to keep its product under constant development. The magnificent engine is now of 5.2 litres rather than 1971's 4.8 and each of the

This V12 feeds a Lamborghini five-speed gearbox that allows nearly 120 mph (192 kph) in third and over 150 mph (240 kph) in fourth. . . . Then you change up for some real speed

cylindric dozen comes with four valves *(quattrovalvole)* per cylinder in place of two.

Naturally, power has increased, but the V12 still wears six twin-choke carburettors rather than fashionable fuel-injection. The chain-activated quartet of overhead camshafts, two per bank of the 60-degree vee, operates in conjunction with a higher compression ratio than the smaller engine possessed (9.5:1) and Magneti Marelli electronic ignition.

The result is an imposing 455 bhp at 7000 rpm while peak torque is 369 lb ft at 5200 revs of the seven-bearing crankshaft. The P112-designated engine has a safe limit of 7500 rpm and has also acted as the base for marine and off-road power units.

This V12 feeds a Lamborghini five-speed gearbox that allows nearly 120 mph (192 kph) in third and over 150 mph (240 kph) in fourth. . . . Then you change up for some real speed! Sharing the rear-drive ZF transaxle with the five gears, is a limited-slip differential and a final-drive ratio that allowed *Autocar* to achieve 179.2 mph (286.7 kph) at just over 7300 fifth-gear revs. The same magazine's two-way average was 178 mph (284.8 kph); 60 mph (96 kph) came up in just 4.9 seconds and the team managed its fastest 0-100 mph (160 kph) run ever in a

Left The most unmistakable supercar silhouette in the world; the Countach has been around since 1971 and still looks spectacular. The slats under the skirts denote this as an '88 model

Below left Tucked away in the centre of the Countach is the superb V12 with four chain-driven cams, and six twin-choke carburettors. Power output is a hugely impressive 455 bhp at 7000 rpm from 5.2 litres

production car, at 10.6 seconds.

Weighing some 3190 lb (1450 kg), the Countach's striking body is made from a tubular-steel chassis and a conglomerate of steel and alloy panels. The car measures 163 inches (4140 mm) in length, and stands on a popular hatchback wheelbase of 96.5 inches (2450 mm). But it is distinguished from the rest of the automotive zoo by its massive, 78.7-inch (2000 mm) width and meagre overall height of just 42.1 inches (1070 mm); you may have to flick up one of the vertically opening doors if you don't want to be overlooked. These doors are unusual, as are the side windows, which rise and fall within a curtailed section. In fact it is more practical to open the door if you want to communicate with the outside world!

The extraordinarily wide wheels and Pirelli's plumpest P7s (345/35VR-15, rear; 225/50, front) hint that equally advanced suspension lies behind the five-hole alloy centres. A conscientiously developed set of wishbones, coil springs, telescopic dampers and appropriate anti-roll bars does the

job, with the dampers doubled up at each rear corner.

The 8.5- and 12-inch x 15-inch Campagnolo alloy wheels are as big as you will find outside Ferrari's newer F40, but they are nearly filled by ventilated disc brakes all round, 11.8 inches (300 mm) in diameter at the front.

Confronted by a speedometer that can register 200 mph

Left On the open road the Countach offers unrivalled performance that sees the 0-100 mph slot covered in just 10.6 seconds, and the chassis handles that power with ease

Below Cramped and claustrophobic; there has to be some price to pay for ultimate supercar performance

(320 kph), it is almost a surprise to find that you start it in just the same way as other, more mundane, vehicles. Once it has been awakened, you are very aware, that more than 5 litres of astoundingly muscular engineering is idling behind your head. But it isn't confined to playing the 7500 rpm wonder car. Despite the need to synchronize six Weber carburettors, it will shuffle into a sub-1000 rpm tickover, and pulling power in top gear is abundant from as low as 1200 rpm.

Apart from the fact that the gearchange is of the competition pattern – first is isolated closest to a LHD pilot – the change itself is not difficult, although the clutch is heavier than is normal today because of the need to withstand the V12's vigour. The steering, too,

requires extra effort, because there is no power assistance in shifting those wide wheels and tyres, which also get in the way of a decently manageable turning circle. But the reward lies in excellent feedback to the driver of the enormous cornering forces generated by such a low and wide machine. Lamborghini offers the car sporting an enormous rear wing that might be seen as an admission of basic instability, but deprived of that speed-robbing appendage the Countach confers absolute confidence to all those lucky enough to steer it.

Does this paragon of performance have any snags? Certainly. Once inside, you feel as though you are trapped in an alien shuttle – one with terrible rearward vision and a rather cramped cabin.

JALPA

LAMBORGHINI

Think of Lamborghini and your mind immediately races to the Countach, that most exotic of exotics with its wailing V12 engine, year-2000 looks and flip-up doors. Certainly the Countach is still a headline stealer, but there is

another car in the 'Lambo' range which, although it may not be as *avant-garde* as its illustrious stablemate, is much more practical and every bit as capable – if not more so!

The Lamborghini Jalpa is the latest in a long line of 'baby Lambos' which dates back to the early 1970s and the strangely titled Urraco. All the cars have been fitted with V8 engines, rather than the more famous V12, and all have been noted for being at the very pinnacle of fine handling and roadholding.

According to legend, wealthy Italian industrialist Ferruccio Lamborghini once purchased a Ferrari and was so disenchanted by its reliability that he decided to build a rival. This he did. He then decided that he would compete with that most famous of

Above The Jalpa is the baby Lamborghini, baby not because of its size (indeed it's larger than its more famous brother the Countach) but because of its smaller, 3.5-litre, engine

Far right The penalty of mid-engined supercar sophistication is an extremely limited view aft over the engine cover and between those buttresses

manufacturers down the road from his Sant' Agata Bolognese factory by producing Lamborghinis for the masses. Hence, in 1970, the mid-engine 2+2 Urraco was born. Styled by Bertone, the new small car, with its 2.5-litre V8 mounted transversely amidships, immediately attracted praise from all for its road manners and practicality. The Press were not quite so convinced about its engine, which featured just one camshaft for each of its two banks of four cylinders, when trends in Italy were tilting towards two per bank.

Much of the Urraco's success

enlarged to a full 3 litres to compete with the 308 GTB Ferrari and each of its cylinder heads was redesigned to accept twin camshafts.

The lacklustre Urracos still failed to attract much custom (there were obviously not enough well heeled masses) so the whole design was opened up – literally. Bertone's brief was to produce a targa-top version of the car and they came up with the Silhouette, which was still powered by that 3-litre, four-cam motor.

By the time the Silhouette arrived, control of the company had passed from Ferruccio to wealthy Swiss recording magnate Patrick Mimram, who saw the future of the small Lamborghini as something else again; in 1981 the Jalpa was born and by 1983 it was

. . . handling and roadholding are second to none, and the big beast really zips through bends and corners like a lightweight with poise, grip and plenty of feel . . .

useless air-conditioning system, but then Lamborghinis are for driving and not for giving 'marks out of ten' in consumer polls.

As the engine revs up and a ratio is selected through that chromium gate, the Jalpa is transformed: the bulk is somehow cast aside and the road starts to flow easily under the wide nose. The radio is just about redundant as at anything like a reasonable gait, so high is the interior noise level, but then, as we have mentioned, part of the car's charm is the thoroughbred note from

depended on the American market and, after that car finally went on sale in the States, the fuel crisis came along and that hit Lamborghini hard. After the company had produced a 2-litre version of the V8 to suit a special tax sector in the Italian market, the 'proper' Urraco had its engine

in production – where it still is today.

Fine leather graces the interior, which helps to justify the price, but quality of finish is only average and wouldn't be tolerated on most production cars. There are many other niggles like poor visibility, stiff controls and almost

those whirring engine internals and that throaty rasp from the exhaust.

The Jalpa's handling and roadholding are second to none, and the big beast really zips through bends and corners like a lightweight, with poise, grip and plenty of feel. There is always

alloy and sitting transversely amidships, where it breathes though a quartet of Weber 42 mm carburettors and produces 255 bhp at 7000 rpm and 231 lb ft of torque at 3500 rpm. Drive passes via a five-speed gearbox to the rear wheels and there is simple MacPherson strut suspension at each corner.

The whole car sits on Campagnolo alloy wheels, which are shod with Pirelli P7 tyres and, as is usual for mid- or rear-engined cars, the tyres at the rear are of slightly larger width than those at

enough power to get this Lambo into trouble when pressing on, but its chassis is set-up to help rather than frighten the driver. A Ford Cosworth Sierra would match the Lamborghini on acceleration, beat it under braking, get fairly close to it on cornering but be some way behind on handling – but then the Ford product costs rather less than the Lamborghini. The Ford also has the benefit of a hatchback, four seats, better economy, and so on.

In the cold light of day, there are many reasons not to choose a Lamborghini Jalpa, but once experienced its Latin brio will convince you that your life isn't complete without one. 'Baby Lamborghini' is really a misnomer, for the Jalpa is bigger in almost every dimension than the Countach, which is substantially wider. However, with just 3.5 litres of engine compared to the Countach's 5.2-litre, 48-valve twelve, it is very much a junior. The power plant is still a gem, though, being built in

Far left & below left Arguably the Jalpa gives you more exclusivity than the Countach; everyone recognizes the Countach's outrageous profile while the Jalpa lines are far harder to place

Left Despite its fine leather trim the Jalpa's interior isn't its strong suit – but then this car is for driving and when the engine starts the quibbles are forgotten and forgiven

the front – 225 mm compared to 205 mm. Steering is by rack and pinion, the rack being situated right under the dashboard so that the actual steering column is incredibly short and thus incredibly positive.

Powerful though the engine is, it needs every one of its horsepower, because the Jalpa weighs a ton and a half (1500 kg), which is much heavier than most average-sized family saloons. Still, the Jalpa can top 145 mph (232 kph) and accelerate to 60 mph (96 kph) in just over 6 seconds. The real penalty is in fuel consumption: you will be lucky to better 19 mpg.

The bulbous Jalpa is perhaps not as elegant as its Silhouette predecessor (of which only 56 examples were constructed) but it will still turn heads anywhere. It doesn't have to be its looks that get it noticed, though, for its exhaust note will announce its arrival long before its buxom form is seen. Although cars have to meet stringent noise-level tests these days, the supercar manufacturers

in Italy seem to get special dispensation. Their cars shriek and wail, but then nobody could deny that it is a wonderful noise!

Compared to that of the claustrophobic Countach, the interior of the Jalpa is positively cavernous, especially when the glassfibre targa top is removed and stowed behind the seats. You sit fairly upright and there is no transmission nor chassis tunnel to get in the way (unlike the spaceframe-chassised Countach, the Jalpa is of unitary monocoque construction). The steering wheel is set high and the pedals offset to the centre of the car, but otherwise the driving position is no problem. Many Lamborghini components, like door locks and switchgear, come from the Fiat parts bin, which somehow gives the cars something of a cheap air (especially when you consider their prices – the Jalpa is more than £44 000). But if Lamborghini were to make their own small items, no doubt the cars would cost substantially more.

S4

LANCIA

Although it won the first of the World Rally Championships it was designed to dominate – November 1985's RAC Rally – the Lancia S4 Delta might well go down in company history as a comparative failure. This exotic machine, created

around the framework of a production Delta hatchback, is one of the few recent Lancia-Abarth rally challengers not to scoop a World Championship title. This has less to do with the car's unique limited-production use of turbo-charging *and* supercharging, than with the

abrupt curtailment, at the close of 1985, of Group B 'supercar' regulations.

Rules that allowed such 450-plus horsepower devices to bound along the rally tracks of the world were inevitably going to cause trouble. The tragedies of the 1985 season affected Lancia particularly,

as two of its works personnel were killed in Corsica at the wheel of an S4: Henri Toivonen and Sergio Cresto.

The S4 Delta carries outward reminders of the Delta production car for marketing purposes, but when it was unveiled at an international press conference in

December 1984, it could be seen that this lightweight three-door, mid-engined, four-wheel drive device had little in common with the steel-bodied five-door hatchback that had inspired its lines since development commenced in April 1983. However, Lancia has since proved that the production Delta can win World Championship rallies, a 250 bhp version of the HF 4WD dominating the 1987 series after Group B was outlawed internationally at the close of 1986.

From the autumn of 1985, Lancia made the 200 S4s necessary to qualify for Group B competition, and a street version of this two-seater competition cocktail went on sale to the public. These cars are not nearly as powerful, nor as light, as the factory rally machines built on the S4 base, but they are still extremely exciting machines.

The S4 engine, displacing 1759 cc, is based on proven Abarth hardware and mounted longitudinally behind the front seats. In the 'production' cars its KKK turbocharger and Abarth Volumex supercharger boost output to a maximum of 250 bhp at 6750 rpm and 214 lb ft of torque. That sounds a lot from less than 1.8 litres, but the similar-sized motor of the Lancia-Martini rally cars was persuaded to yield a reliable 470 bhp at 8000 revs, plus more than 333 lb ft of torque.

The aim of using both a turbo unit and supercharging was to overcome the lazy low-speed response of the turbo. The supercharger looks after the provision of extra punch below about 3500 revs, and the

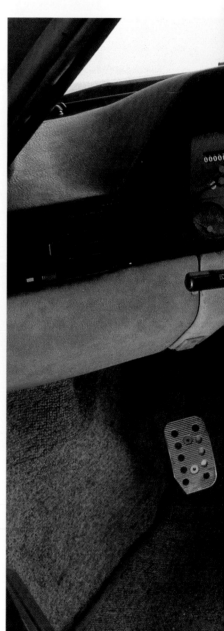

turbocharger supplies an increasing amount of boost at higher rpm.

The competition S4 used exactly the same twin intercooler principles, but the transition from supercharging to turbocharging took place at higher engine speeds, between 5000 and 6000 revs. Developing the engine's mechanically driven supercharger and the exhaust-impelled turbo to the point where power and torque delivery were harmonious was a complex challenge. Fiat-Lancia-Abarth engineers eventually met it successfully, but as yet nobody else has repeated the experiment . . .

Both competition and road derivatives of this extraordinary design have been based on a chrome-molybdenum steel-tube frame in a two-seater cabin reinforced by box-section structures; these also serve as the main north-south chassis. Epoxy resins with glassfibre reinforcement provide the bulk of the external panels on the road car. The factory rally S4s used flyweight carbonfibre composites for items such as the 'bonnet', slashing kerb weight from a roadgoing 2640 lb (1200 kg) to less than 2200 lb (1000 kg).

Just as complex as the engine bay full of tubes, coolers and Marelli-Weber ignition/injection management is the 4WD system. The bulk of the central transmission is mounted forward of the four-cylinder engine and is packed with features including a five-speed gearbox, a Ferguson viscous-coupled limited-slip

Above From the front the S4 looks disarmingly conventional and ordinary – that's an illusion

each side of the rear suspension, gas-damped by Bilstein on the competition S4s.

Because of the high power outputs achieved during this 'supercar' era of rallying, power steering became common equipment in top-flight cars. The Lancia uses pneumatic assistance for its rack-and-pinion steering that skips from lock to lock in just 2.5 turns. Even on the production cars, a quartet of massive 11.8-inch diameter disc brakes are deployed front and rear.

Above Only Lancia so far have managed to combine successfully both turbocharging and supercharging on the same engine, extracting some 470 bhp from 1759 cc of intercooled twin-cam

Right The genuine article, the S4 of Lancia works driver Markku Alen

differential and epicyclic gears to split power thirty per cent front, seventy per cent rear. The back axle carries a conventional multiplate, limited-slip differential.

The description above applies to the cars sold to the public at more than £40 000; the works rally cars used a variety of traction enhancement devices and power splits to suit terrain from tarmac to sheet ice. Typical of the expensive lengths to which they would go was the fitment of titanium drive shafts in place of the road car's beefy steel units: every ounce counted.

Suspension and brake design is equally sophisticated and akin to a sports-racing car in the use of double wishbones and links. For rough road rallying plenty of cushioning is needed, so double telescopic dampers are fitted on

. . . enduring memories are of the S4's astonishing grip and braking and its inspired acceleration . . . more important is its ability to jink over tight Mediterranean trails . . .

Pirelli supplied some very special 205/55 VR tyres that bear different tread patterns across their width to complement the car's suspension under varying loads. To accommodate those huge brakes, elegant Speedline alloy wheels of 16-inch diameter and 8-inch rim width are standard equipment.

Although the cars were created purely for competition, the public-sale S4s are trimmed in Alcantra cloth, and cope easily with everyday traffic conditions. The cabin boasts comprehensive instrumentation in the Lancia tradition, including a 260 kph (163 mph) speedometer and 9000 rpm tachometer, red-lined at 7500 for public road use.

Driving the car, it is initially the assistance of those two whining compressors, alongside double overhead camshafts and the sixteen-valve cylinder head, that make the greater impression. However, enduring memories are of the S4's astonishing grip and braking and its inspired acceleration – 0-62 mph (100 kph) in 6.0 seconds. Lancia reckon that the road car will reach 140 mph (224 kph), but more important is its ability to jink over tight Mediterranean trails at a glorious 7200 rpm, allowing 65 mph (104 kph) in second and 92 mph (147 kph) in third.

Riding alongside works drivers such as Markku Alen in the 470 horsepower rally car was something else. Inside that stark cockpit all you could do was watch in awe as impossible feats were achieved by a man and machine beyond mere mortal comprehension.

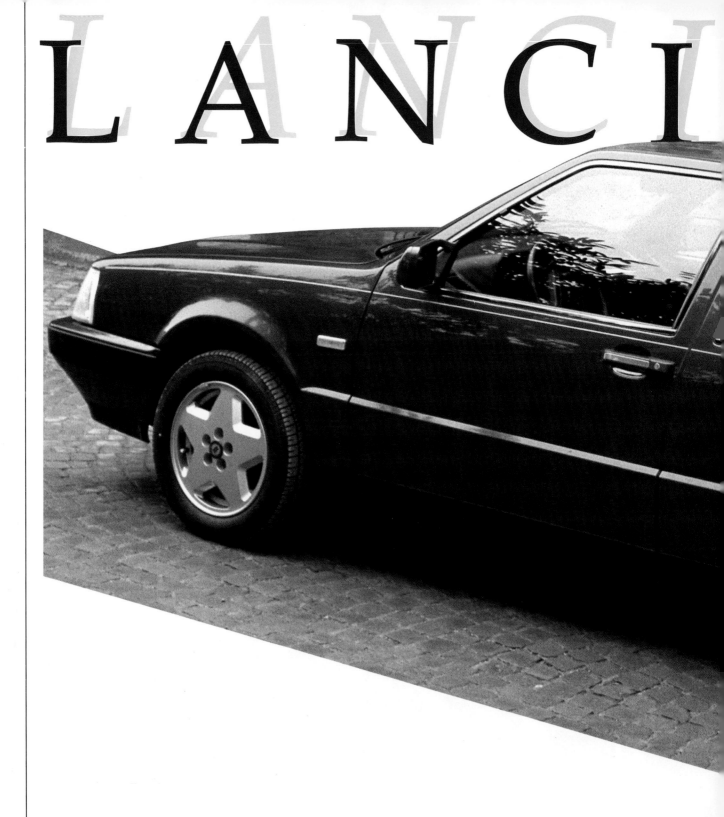

THEMA 8.32 FERRARI
LANCIA

The combination of Ferrari power and Lancia bodywork has provided the owner of both concerns, Fiat, with a number of memorable winners in World Championship rallying and sports car racing. Yet the accommodating four-door saloon now perpetuating the alliance

had no sporting purpose about its conception.

Officially labelled Lancia Thema 8.32, and nicknamed the 'Lancia-Ferrari', this version of the Lancia saloon was designed to compete in the class of swift executive expresses. While the rest of the Fiat-owned Lancia range competes against marques such

as Audi, the 149 mph (238 kph), limited-production Thema, at £30 000-plus, stands out as the flagship, and competes against sombre-suited machines with 286 horsepower hearts, such as BMW's M5.

Although the 8.32 Thema might seem a logical Fiat Group alliance, it actually took all the political

influence of Fiat director Vittorio Ghidella to realize the union of the Thema with Ferrari's eight-cylinder, thirty-two-valve (thus '8.32') V8. Sig Ghidella ensured that one of Lancia's traditional Torinese homes for performance cars was rejuvenated to hand-build the cars. Fittingly, this special Thema, with its disappearing rear

Its front-drive, five-speed transaxle now had to withstand . . . more than 200 lb ft of pulling power and there were many who thought the result would be a very twitchy car . . .

wing, was first shown to the public at the April 1986 Turin Motor Show.

While the bulk of the Thema is Lancia, albeit modified in key areas to cope with the large increase in power, the alloy V8 is pure Ferrari.

Naturally much of the running gear of the old flagship – 2-litre 165 bhp Thema Turbo – had to be as thoroughly overhauled as the old Lancia factory.

Its front-drive, five-speed transaxle now had to withstand Ferrari's 215 bhp and more than 200 lb ft of pulling power, and there were many who thought the result would be a very twitchy car indeed, particularly over slippery surfaces. Lancia appears to have confounded them all,

Right & below
Almost everything about the fastest Thema is understated; the 'Lancia by Ferrari' engine gives no hint that under its plain cover is a 215 bhp alloy V8 while the Thema body gives little clue to its performance

although four-wheel drive has always been planned for this model, along with electronically adjustable damper characteristics.

The engine is the same as that used by Ferrari in the mid-engined 308 coupés and fresh-air spyders; the company switched to a 3.2-litre version of the 90-degree V8 for the appropriately tagged 328. The 2927 cc unit compactly packages many advanced features, including four valves per cylinder and double overhead camshafts on each cylinder bank.

Incidentally, the engine was detuned for the Thema, the power output dropping from 240 bhp at 7000 rpm to the quoted 215 bhp at 6750 rpm, but the torque figure was enhanced, to 209 lb ft at 4500 revs – more suitable for hauling a spacious four-door that weighs over 2800 lb (1400 kg)

Apart from a stronger transmission, other Thema modifications made to cater for the extra 50 bhp include new components for the four-wheel MacPherson strut suspension. New lower front suspension wishbones were made and the springs/dampers were re-calibrated to work correctly with the front and rear anti-roll bars.

West Germany's ZF concern supplies the 'Servotronic' power steering that does much to calm the feedback from the oversized aluminium wheels. Covered by plump 205/55-section Goodyear Eagle tyres, the five-spoke wheels measure a generous 6 x 15 inches. Behind those distinctive alloys lurk four-wheel disc brakes, ventilated for the front only but equipped with Bosch anti-lock electronics as standard.

Body changes to the Thema (which originated from a 'Type 4' co-development with Saab, Lancia and Alfa Romeo) are modest. A sharp eye might detect the extra spoiler depth at the front or the side skirting which carries the 8.32 badges but the most understated item of all is the rear wing, which folds away inside the boot when not required. Experienced drivers report that they can tell little difference in the Thema's manners with the wing extended or folded away. . . .

In the large cabin obvious

Right As speed
increases the boot
mounted rear wing
extends to keep the
Thema's rear firmly
attached to the road;
in reality it's the
Lancia's one
concession to
gimmickry

Far right Lancia
have gone the
Jaguar route of black
leather and wood
trimming with the
interior

modifications have been made. The wood trim on door cappings and fascia suggests that Lancia is aiming at Jaguar-type luxury as well as prestige and speed, an impression reinforced by the padded three-spoke steering wheel, a wide selection of round dials and leather trim on luxuriously appointed seating.

Wielding that power-assisted steering, you are aware that this is a big machine (15 ft/4.59 m in length), but the light touch needed to operate all the major controls makes it an easy car to control, even in city traffic. The Ferrari engine makes its presence audibly apparent – with an engine note slightly deeper than Ferrari's usual soprano trilling – but its advanced electronics and injection ensure that it has none of the urban hiccups associated with a racing heritage.

The emphasis on less horsepower and greater mid-range muscle pays dividends: the 8.32 is happy to demonstrate its good-natured speed from 30 to 100 mph (48 to 160 kph) in fourth and fifth gears.

Flat out, Lancia reckons on 149 mph (240 kph) and 0-62 mph (100 kph) in less than 7 seconds. That top speed is about the same as in the old BMW M5, but the weight and power curve prevents acceleration lower down from matching that of the German car; higher up the range, the Thema's comparatively clean lines (0.32 Cd) allow its 0-100 mph (160 kph) times to compare favourably with the opposition.

Fuel consumption usually averages around 20 mpg, but the Thema handles with so much more assurance than was originally anticipated that less than 20 mpg is more likely for enthusiastic users.

All who drive the Thema are pleasantly surprised at how capably it handles so much front-end power and weight, with sixty-two per cent of its 3080 lb (1400 kg) being forward of the centre line. In fact, this example of the successful combination of power and space has been one of the high spots of 1980s motoring.

LOTUS

ESPRIT S4

LOTUS

When it was first produced, in June 1976, the 135 mph (216.kph) Lotus Esprit reflected perfectly the heritage of the Lotus Grand Prix team. Features such as the four-valve-per-cylinder engine mounted amidships, glassfibre

body over steel chassis and four-wheel disc brakes (then inboard at the rear, as was racing practice) made the Esprit unique.

This, combined with Lotus's prowess at producing both plastic bodies and supreme sporting suspension systems, resulted in a car which had few rivals outside

the Porsche and Ferrari class.

The 1987 Series 4 (S4) Esprit incorporates those advanced features, many of them further developed, in a completely new body that was successfully and transatlantically debuted in the autumn of 1987. The original Esprit style was developed by the

late Colin Chapman (the Lotus genius died in December 1982) and Italy's internationally acclaimed designer, Giorgio Giugiaro. The 1987 body, still a strict two-door two-seater, benefited from outside design assistance, but was primarily the work of Lotus Cars employees under the leadership of design director Colin Spooner.

As has been the case since the June 1980 debut of a turbocharged Esprit, the S4 is available with or without turbocharging. In either case the basic engine is Lotus's aluminium four-cylinder unit, with a double-overhead-camshaft cylinder head carrying sixteen valves. At the time of its introduction, in 1972, this layout was almost exclusively confined to racing cars, so all credit must go to Lotus for developing it for production. The engine was enlarged from its original 2 litres, generating 140 bhp, in Jensen and Lotus products to 2.2 litres by 1979.

This larger size (2174 cc to be precise) was the result of a joint effort with Talbot to provide an engine capable of powering a World Rally Championship contender. And that is exactly what the cumbersomely named Talbot Sunbeam Lotus 2.2 achieved in 1981, developing 155 bhp for public sale or 240 bhp in competition tune. The 2.2-litre capacity first appeared in Lotus cars via the 1980 Esprit Turbo and is in use throughout the model range, which includes a front-mounted version in the Excel.

The S4 Esprit offers 172 bhp at 6500 rpm in twin carburetted form, or 215 bhp at 6000 rpm from the Garrett AiResearch turbocharged unit. The curvaceous 1987 body offsets this against a slight increase in weight to leave overall Esprit performance much as before, the £22 950 Esprit S4 reaching a claimed 138 mph (221 kph) and the £28 900 Turbo

From the driving seat, facing the leather-trimmed, two-spoke steering wheel, the S4's improvements can be summarized as a little more of everything . . .

using its extra power and torque to record a reported 152 mph (245 kph). Yet straight-line speed – the Turbo sprints to 60 mph (96 kph) in a scant 5.3 seconds, its cheaper cousin in 6.5 – is far from the sole reason that the Esprit holds such a strong fascination.

For the traditional Lotus World Class standards of handling and grip remain, but are here allied to important new creature comforts. Lotus has instilled civilized noise levels into a retrimmed cabin that is separated from the engine by a bulkhead in marine ply and the automotive equivalent of double glazing. A stiffer body structure, with bonded glass, makes the 1987 Esprit cockpit far quieter than its predecessors.

Left An in-house Lotus design has replaced the Giugiaro styling of the previous car. Although the lines of the S4 are far softer and rounded the dimensions are almost exactly those of the sharp-edged S3.

Below 2.2 litres of turbocharged twin-cam produces 172 bhp, enough to power the S4 to 152 mph

Externally only a few minor items (door handles, for example) are carried over from earlier Esprits. The body rests over the usual galvanized steel chassis 'backbone', deploying composite fibre technologies such as Kevlar reinforcement.

The bodyshell and all major exterior panels are produced by a refined version of the Lotus-patented process VARI, by which body halves are amalgamated without the old 'seams' that were emphasized by the sharply edged styles of the seventies. Even the

broad 7 x 15-inch (front) and 8 x 15-inch (rear) Lotus-styled and Italian-made alloy wheels are completely new.

To tell the difference between turbocharged and non-turbo Esprits, start at the 'glassback' extra rear window on the turbocharged model, which makes it even more difficult to see what is directly behind you. Other exterior distinguishing points include matt black mirrors on the 172 bhp car,

rather than the Turbo's body-colour units, and those with sharper eyes will be able to pick out rear-end dissimilarities in the number plate surround and under-bumper valance, plus differences in the air intakes at the nose. Of necessity the turbocharged Esprit has always featured careful air management

Right The rear view shows how subtle have been the changes from S3 to S4

Above right The luxury of two-tone soft leather trim is optional

within its engine bay, assisted by the now considerably less noticeable intakes ahead of the rear window, and functional scoops integrated on the bottom sills, ahead of the rear wheels.

Important mechanical advances include a five-speed Renault 25-sourced gearbox to replace the original Citroën SM item, although American production began without this mechanical modification. All models feature repositioned disc brakes (now conventionally mounted at the outboard end of the rear driveshafts), lightweight wiring and stainless-steel exhaust systems.

From the driving seat, facing the leather-trimmed, two-spoke (three on Turbo models) steering wheel, the S4's improvements can be summarized as a little more of everything: space, trim, information and comfort. The fascia is populated by five traditional black and white dials with clearly marked push buttons within easy reach at either end of the binnacle's curve. According to model, the trim may be leather or cloth, or even a combination of both.

In action the turbocharged Esprit has traded some of its immediate impact for a softer and more civilized approach. The turbocharger installation was always one of the best in the world for instant response, relying on the finned induction intake rather than the plumbing associated with an air radiator (intercooler) to cool the incoming charge. The motor remains happy to growl through town or country. It will untemperamentally run through

Far left There's nothing flamboyant or flashy about the Turbo Esprit S4's instrumentation, just the necessary information displayed in the proper analogue fashion

Left The vent below the rear window discharges the hot air from the turbo engine

the five gears from low revs, but is at its most inspired between 4000 and 7000 rpm, when it propels the low cabin forward at the rate that many light aircraft cannot match.

Over the bumps and ripples of the Lotus test track at Hethel in Norfolk, the new Esprit remains unflurried and comfortable at simply enormous cornering speeds. If there is a faster way of getting around corners, we probably will not see it until Lotus itself unveils its next generation of microprocessor-managed active suspension cars.

These machines will prove that racing can benefit the public road breed – a lesson not lost on Lotus Cars, even though the company is now owned by the world's biggest corporation, General Motors. Incidentally, the Grand Prix Lotus team continues under separate private ownership, including that of Hazel Chapman, the founder's widow.

LYNX

D-TYPE
LYNX

Jaguar are now firmly back at the top of the sports-car-racing ladder, a position they were last in some thirty years ago. Three decades of racing-car design have seen plenty of changes, of course, but the Jaguars still use production-based engines as did their historic

stabilizing fin running to the rear from behind the driver's head. First raced in 3-litre form, the D-types managed around 170 mph (272 kph) on the long Mulsanne straight – when they ran 3441 cc.

Lynx Engineering, of St Leonards-on-Sea on the Sussex coast, are Jaguar specialists, and their busy workshops are full of cars being restored, engines being tuned and their own cars being built. They make conversions for Jaguar XJ-S coupés – either estates or dropheads. However, Lynx are most famous for the D-type, which is a loving re-creation of the famous 1950s racer.

The Lynx is based around E-type mechanicals, indeed the finished car is classed as a rebodied E-type Jaguar. The E-type subframes are used, joined by a central tub and clothed in a lovingly crafted body

hat-trick of Le Mans races from 1955 to '57. The D-type was the most modern racer of its day; its gorgeously contoured aluminium body was actually its chassis, a fully stressed monocoque. What looked like a rail chassis in the engine bay and through the cockpit was in fact an alloy subframe to which the engine and suspension was attached and which was secured to the back of the tub, ahead of the rear axle.

The car's body was as sleek as it was attractive and it was easily recognizable with its large

predecessors.

The D-type was the successor to the C-type, the purpose-built racer with which Jaguar twice won the classic Le Mans 24-hour race. The newer car had a look about it which rightly backed up the adage that 'what looks right, is right'. The D-type proved that by winning a

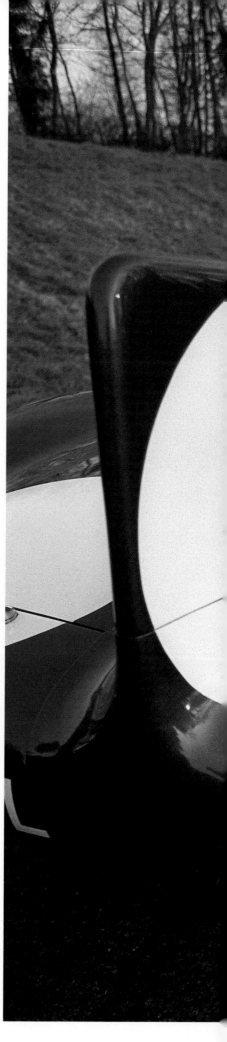

made of 16 swg aluminium and riveted into place. The actual final look of the car can be as varied as any of the 71 D-types which were built. It can have either a short, slow-circuit nose, or a swoopier and longer Le Mans nose. It can have a full width windscreen with two passenger places or a single wrap-around 'screen with a metal tonneau cover over the passenger compartment. And the exhaust can be routed either to exit at the rear or from the flanks. Indeed, if you really want, Lynx will dispense with the E-type parts and build a complete D, but in Britain at least this could lead to type-approval problems. If, however, the thought of a Lynx resembling a car of which 71 originals were built is too common for you, then you can order yours as an XKSS. Just sixteen of these two-seater road cars were produced from unwanted D-type chassis at the factory before a fire stopped production. They were fitted with a full windscreen, extra interior trim, a luggage rack and a hood.

The options are either 3.8 or 4.2-litre XK motors . . . tuning can raise the power to well over 300 bhp which is more than most of the original racers had

They are much rarer than the racers and much more valuable.

Lynx will fit a Jaguar engine with as much performance as you could want. The options are either 3.8 or 4.2-litre XK motors in standard form, but tuning can raise the power to well over 300 bhp, which is more than most of the original racers had.

Lynx go to a lot of trouble to make sure that the detailing of their cars is right and they even make the replica 16-in wheels themselves, which is no easy task for a small engineering company. The dimensions mostly mirror the original with only the bonnet rising slightly more than normal to cover the E-type engine, which is wet- rather than dry-sumped like the racers.

From every angle, the Lynx is pure thoroughbred. The finish of the hand-beaten aluminium body is the work of the finest craftsmen and the riveting harks back to a time gone by when cars were built up to a quality and not down to a price. From the cockpit, the year could be 1957, with large central gauges reading engine and road speed and minor dials spread liberally across the rest of the dashboard, behind the aluminium-spoked and wood-rimmed steering wheel, monitoring the rest of the car's functions.

A large gear lever sprouts from

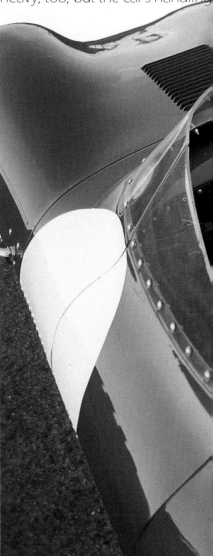

the transmission tunnel and points forward, while a chromium handbrake is slotted down by the side. You sit low in the Lynx, though, with just your head protruding over the line of the top of the perspex 'screen. The engine fires and idles raucously, its exhaust system designed primarily to aid gas flow rather than to take any sting out of the noise of the big six up ahead. The controls are heavy but the car springs forward from rest much as a feline Jaguar would when startled.

The steering is positive, if a little heavy, too, but the car's handling

on its tall, thin tyres is sharp and the car feels like a racer. Where the Lynx really differs from the original is in that the rear suspension, being from the E-type, is independent, whereas the live-axled Jaguar D-types had a reputation for providing a hard ride and nervous handling on bumpy roads. Not so the Sussex car, for its ride is supple and forgiving. However, if you wish to keep *everything* original, Lynx will be happy to supply a solid rear axle!

Even with a standard engine, the lightweight Lynx is a real flyer, and it is strange having such supercar performance available from 'only' a six-cylinder engine up ahead. However, the classic Jaguar XK motor is no ordinary six, and it gives the D-type high performance from low or high revs in all gears. Given a full-house tuning job, you can bank on a top speed of over 160 mph (256 kph) and 0-60 mph (96 kph) acceleration in well under 6 seconds!

Lynx D-types are not cheap, costing anything from £45 000 upwards, but then a real Jaguar D-type will cost a lot more on top

of that. The newer car matches if not betters the original in most respects of construction and performance (three decades of engineering evolution has seen to that), but obviously cannot hope to compete with the Jaguar in terms of charisma. Perhaps the only solution is to be like the Japanese businessman who recently put his genuine article 'D' into the workshops for restoration. When it goes home, it will share a garage with a Lynx D-type which is absolutely identical, even down to the stickers. This man drives the Lynx on the busy roads at home, not worrying if it should get knocked, and uses the Jaguar for special occasions like the Mille Miglia. He at least knows that he has the best of both worlds!

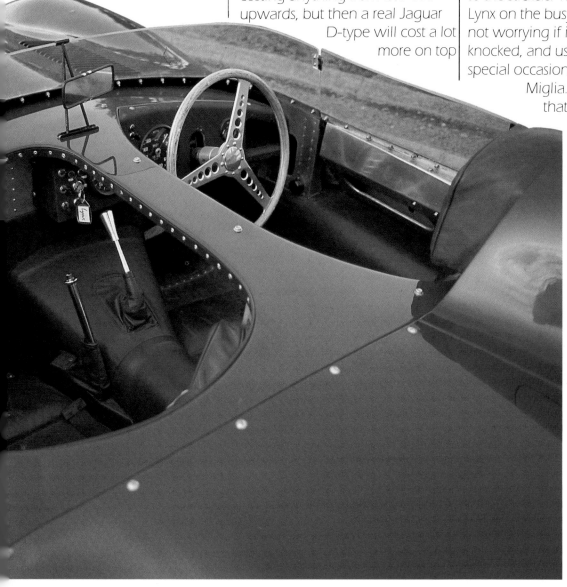

The Lynx's sleek curves follow exactly those drawn by the D-type's stylist Malcolm Sayer to speed the car down the Mulsanne Straight at Le Mans

MANTULA SPYDER

MARCOS

If a Marcos Mantula were to sweep past as you stood gawping at the kerbside, you would remark that it looked fast, very fast, as well as stylish and modern. Strange then that you could have been on that same kerbside and seen a very similar car swoop past

almost a quarter of a century before!

The Marcos GT first saw the light of day back in 1963, and it astounded as much for its construction as for its appearance, which, then as now, was looked on as ultra futuristic. The Marcos name is an amalgam of those of Jem MARsh, who still runs the company, and Frank COStin who designed the early machines which Jem then put together. Frank Costin had made his name as an aerodynamicist, first in the aircraft industry and then in car racing, and it was he who clothed the famous Vanwall Grand Prix car, which also featured a Colin Chapman-designed chassis.

As well as being an engineer gifted in the art of streamlining, Frank was also a brilliant chassis man with a soft spot for wood as a suitable material. Thus, the early forerunners to the GT had marine-ply frames, which meant that they

. . . with some 190 bhp and 220 lb ft of torque available in Vitesse form, there is no shortage of oomph available . . . the dash from 0-60 mph takes under 6 seconds . . .

were light, strong and ultra durable. Jem used a marine-ply chassis for the early GTs, too, but switched to steel frames in 1970 due to the prohibitive cost of the wood. This meant that the last link with Costin had gone, for the styling of the GT was in fact carried out by Dennis Adams, a point which was missed by many then and is still missed by many now.

Over the years, the GT has been powered by a variety of engines – four-cylinder Fords, of both straight and vee design, Volvos of four and six cylinders, a V6 Ford and now a Rover V8. Jem Marsh hasn't been building his classic sportsters non stop, however, for the fuel crisis in the early 1970s saw production halted and the company sold. It was only when Jem got back into servicing his older cars and talking to Marcos enthusiasts, that he realized there would be a market for the cars again, so in 1981 he decided to revive the car whose look is as famous as any in the world of British sports cars.

Jem called upon Dennis Adams to adapt the front of the car to make it lower and thus cover up the deep radiator of the Rover engine, and he obtained confirmation from Austin-Rover that there would be a plentiful supply of their V8 for many years to come. The next big step for the Mantula, as the car with its V8

Left *The Mantula Spyder retains much of the look of the Dennis Adams-styled Marcos GT of 1963 with suitable modifications such as the rear spoiler (far left) to enable it to deal with the performance given by its V8 engine*

power was christened, was for Jem to take its top off, something that has literally opened up a whole new market for the Wiltshire wonder now that dropheads are back in vogue. Dennis Adams was again called upon to do the trick, and such is the success of his revamped design that the Marcos looks for all the world as if it was intended to be a convertible from day one.

The Mantula Spyder, like the ordinary Mantula, uses a square-section-steel chassis, consisting of a deep perimeter frame with plenty of bracing. Because part of the Mantula's strength comes from the all-enclosing glassfibre outer bodywork, the chassis of the drophead has to be strengthened with sheet-metal and extra-tube bracing in certain areas. However, considering that when you sit in a Marcos the uppermost chassis frame member runs transversely at about neck level, the car is not lacking in rigidity.

All Spyders actually start off as hardtops (it is much easier to mould them that way); then the required cutting is done and

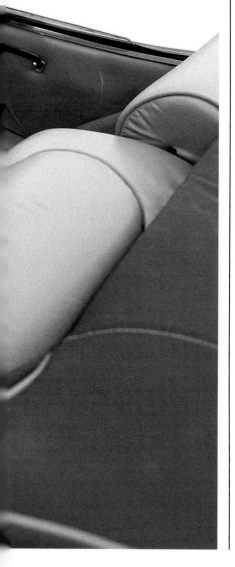

the soft-top attached. The rear view of any Marcos is always the least attractive angle, but the Spyder suffers more than the rest with its 'blind' rear-three-quarter panels. In other directions that deep, be-spoilered nose only adds to the charm of the Marcos look.

Suspension at the front of the car is Triumph based (as has been the case for many British specialist sports cars – including the fabled Lotus Elan), while that at the rear is designed to attach the sturdy Ford Capri back axle. The Rover engine which Jem employs is the fuel-injected motor from the Rover Vitesse. Although many users of this superb, all-alloy motor tune them to produce astonishing amounts of power, Mr Marsh believes in keeping the unit standard; but with some 190 bhp and 220 lb ft of torque available in Vitesse form, there is no shortage of oomph available. Top speed works out at around 140 mph (224 kph), while the dash from 0 to 60 mph (96 kph) takes under 6 seconds, which is supercar quick.

Standing just 42.5 in (108 mm) high, the Marcos is not an easy car to get into, but once in you lie almost prone and are squeezed gently by the large transmission tunnel and the comfortable, fixed seats. Fixed? How does the car adjust to different-size passengers, then? There is a knurled knob on the dashboard, which when turned moves a frame in the footwell to carry the pedals in and out. This means that the seats can be neatly integrated with the rear bulkhead and the floor and just makes the leather-clad interior look that bit more attractive. With

walnut for the dashboard, as is customary for British sporting cars, the Marcos interior is very attractive indeed.

Smaller drivers may still find the view out a little awkward, especially over that long, swooping bonnet, but the Mantula is not a very large car, so it is quite easy to guide. The Rover V8 gives it smooth, easy performance in any of its five gears and a real solid punch away from rest. The steering is precise if rather heavy, especially as the layout demands a straight-arm driving position, and the car handles like a dream. With drivers of the calibre of Jackie Stewart, Derek Bell and, more recently, Jonathan Palmer, having raced Marcoses and Jem himself still campaigning one successfully, the car's manners are bound to be refined – and they are. The Mantula is a very well sorted car and makes full use of the grip available from its 225-section tyres.

With the top down, the Mantula Spyder still permits motoring in comfort at three-figure speeds, due to the low driving position and the way the air swoops over rather than into the cockpit. Given a warm, summer's day, an empty sinewy country road and hefty helpings of throttle, the car will give you a wonderful drive at speeds which few other cars could match.

The Marcos Mantula may have a history stretching back a quarter-century, but it goes to prove that what was good then can still be good now. Steady honing has proved in this case that evolution is as good as revolution.

BITURBO SPYDER

MASERATI

C osting £28 795 in winter
1987/8, the Maserati Biturbo
Spyder (meaning it is a twin
turbocharger convertible) is
a rarity on British roads. It
has all the glamour of Italian
exotica, but is more practical than
most, equipped with a flexible V6
engine, convenient hood

operation and plenty of luggage space for the two occupants.

The Biturbo Maseratis were launched in Italy during the autumn of 1981 as 2-litre cars, but by 1983 a 2.5-litre version of the unusual V6 was also available. Unfortunately, the establishment of an effective British dealer network proved more difficult than the mechanical modification of the widely praised car.

It was 1986 before the Maserati marque was re-established in Britain; and during the following year the fact of a take-over and new management had to be absorbed before the twenty-one appointed British retailers could get on with the job. These delays were unfortunate because by the time its RHD format was established, the Maserati was beginning to look a little dated; yet there was still plenty of interest from loyal and patient admirers of the drophead derivative.

The Biturbo principle of fitting a turbocharger to serve each bank of the 90-degree V6 has been applied to three body styles: two-door coupé; 425 four-door saloon and the Spyder convertible manufactured by Zagato of Milan. These use the original 2-litre engine at a carburetted 180 bhp, or the electronically fuel-injected 2.5-litre unit yielding as much as 220 horsepower. The convertible for British sale slots into the middle of that spectrum, boasting 192 bhp generated via assistance from a Weber double-choke carburettor.

Although its front-engined, rear-drive nature suggests an utterly conventional car, the Maserati's engine bay is crowded with features even more novel than the application of twin turbochargers from the IHI Corporation in Japan.

Each of the alloy-construction V6's two-cylinder heads runs a single overhead camshaft serving *three* valves per cylinder. This design feature is not uncommon in Japanese motorcycles and cars, Toyota and Honda being the primary exponents among mass-production car makers. Yet the configuration of a single exhaust valve and two intakes had not been employed anywhere else in Europe when Maserati adopted the system.

The twin turbos and eighteen valves are complemented by an electronic boost-control system which ensures that the 7.4:1 compression engine is not over-boosted at any point in the engine rpm range. In the Spyder's case, maximum power is restricted to

192 bhp at 5500 rpm and a fat 220 lb ft of torque, because the boost provided by both turbos is restrained to a modest 0.8 bar.

Such extensive engine-bay technology is aimed at reducing the time it takes the turbochargers to respond to increased throttle ('turbo lag'), and most independent reporters feel Maserati has succeeded in providing an extraordinarily smooth flow of power.

The Maserati is not a particularly fast car on its twin turbo V6, *Autocar* having measured a maximum of 128 mph (206 kph) and 0-60 mph (96 kph) in 7.2 seconds. Rather, the Italian company has set out to provide strong and relaxed mid-range performance that proves particularly useful when overtaking. The penalty for such prompt turbocharger action is that the driver is tempted to use the boosted horsepower more frequently than in many other contemporary installations, so that fuel consumption can be dragged well below 20 mph.

Moving the spotlight away from 'on-paper' performance figures, the convertible 'Maser' offers a number of other benefits. To achieve the rakish air favoured by convertible drivers, Zagato has shortened the Spyder's wheelbase from the Biturbo coupé's 102 inches (2600 mm) to 94 inches (2400 mm). Overall length has dropped from the Biturbo coupé's 164 inches (4155 mm) to 159 inches (4040 mm), and the official kerb weight is also down, the Spyder being quoted at 2387 lb (1085 kg).

*Maserati set out to establish
the Biturbo Spyder as a gentleman's
fast tourer rather than as a sports car,
avoiding a rock hard ride
and rorty engine manners*

Maserati set out to establish the Biturbo Spyder as a gentleman's fast tourer rather than as a sports car, avoiding a rock-hard ride and rorty engine manners. One of its main attractions is the unusually expensive finish of its convertible

Left Twin turbos help the three-valve-per-cylinder engine produce 192 bhp

Below The drophead body is by Zagato

cabin. Leather upholstery is sometimes avoided in soft-top designs for fear of a sudden drenching, but Maserati has used hide for the seats, doors, fascia and for the rim of the four-spoke steering wheel.

Seated on one of the two seats provided (there is not even a token attempt at a 'plus-two' rear parcel shelf), the Biturbo Spyder driver is soothed by walnut wood finish and air conditioning. Electric windows and power steering continue the list of creature comforts, but the highlight is a natty timepiece that looks as if it has come from an Italian design house: it is an ovoid curiosity in the centre of the dashboard.

Instrumentation is comprehensive in the Italian sporting manner: seven dials monitor functions, from the engine rpm red line of 6400 to the boost achieved by those twin turbochargers.

The suspension is a straightforward configuration of front MacPherson struts and independent rear trailing arms. A concession to improved traction is one of the earliest European uses of the Torsen (TORque SENsing) limited-slip differential, a device which has latterly been more widely employed by Audi and Lancia in combination with all-wheel-drive.

At the wheel, the taller driver will be aware that the car was designed with the Italian driving position in mind, but the amiable engine and five-speed gearbox allow easy access to power.

Despite the fitment of front and rear anti-roll bars, a good deal of

body lean is evident in hard cornering – more proof that Maserati was aiming at touring rather than sports car customers.

The grip provided by the Michelin MXV tyres of 205 section on plump alloy rims of 6.5 inches beam is certainly above average. Also well above the norm are the generous dimensions of the vacuum servo-assisted brakes:

11.1-inch (282 mm), front and 10.7-inch (272 mm), rear.

By the time the Maserati Biturbos arrived in Britain, much of their initial attraction had been diluted thanks to price and modest engine capacity. Nevertheless, they marked a welcome reappearance in Britain of an Italian marque that has always been noted for distinctive design.

MG

METRO 6R4

Another exotic cocktail based upon a production outline for the 'Golden Age' of rallying, the Metro 6R4 continued to cause sporting excitement long after production ceased in 1985. Although it never did win a round of the World Rally Championship, for which it was conceived (neither did the Ford RS200), the winged and bug-like Metro went on winning consistently in British rally and rallycross championship

events in the late 1980s. The agile Metro's successful competition antics finally led to the creation of a British Championship rally series specifically for this, the most exotic of all Metros.

'Exotic' and 'Metro', surely they do not belong in the same sentence? On the contrary, such an adjective is fitting for a Metro whose heart has been scalloped away and replaced with a V6 competition engine, capable of transmitting over 400 bhp to an advanced all-wheel-drive system. The official price was more than £40 000 initially, but many were sold off at the end of 1986 for less than £20 000 – recognized competitors paying considerably less than that.

Incidentally, the '6' in the name refers to the number of cylinders in that purpose-built alloy engine, the 'R' stands for Rally, and the '4' is for four-wheel-drive (4WD). The advanced power unit was not an adaptation of any existing Austin Rover or Honda engine, but was designed by the company's own Motorsport department at Cowley under the leadership of David Wood. Inside the company the unit was referred to as the V64V, which simply meant it was a V6 with four valves per cylinder.

Only 200 such Metros were constructed by Britain's state-owned car maker, and most were originally made in 'Clubman' tune, which had a lower power output than that quoted above. Unlike

For the public the Metro 6R4 story began when the first 'concept car' was driven dramatically through a cinema screen at a West London press conference. Painted the emotive red and white of the old Abingdon Mini Coopers that had conquered the world's most prestigious rallies, the rally version of the Metro naturally aroused patriotic fervour.

The basic layout of 4WD and a mid-mounted V6 unit (then a

... the 90 degree V6 designed by the Motorsport department was sufficiently powerful and reliable to take the car to third place in its debut event ...

Above *A bizarre mixture of production components (like the Montego steering wheel) and competition items like the seats combine uneasily in the 6R4*

Right *The Metro 6R4 may not have had much chance to show its metal in Group B but its career continued successfully in lesser rally classes*

many rivals, who subcontracted output of their competition cars to specialist sports personnel, or outside factories, Austin Rover's mass-production Longbridge factory in Birmingham was the site for the 6R4's assembly. However, the works rally entries, as for any serious factory competition car, were stripped and built from bare shells in the sports department.

As its bulging outline suggests, the Metro 6R4 shared few components with a production Metro. The factory quoted '374 unique panels', plus 'a further sixteen panels' as used on the standard Metro. . . . Of the basic body parts, only the roll cages were not made inside Austin Rover. Just how much skilled handiwork was demanded can be judged by the fact that over 137 ft (41.8 metres) of welding was required, compared to 4 ft (1.2 metres) on a standard Metro.

Rover V8 minus two cylinders) was executed by Williams Engineering at Didcot to an Austin Rover Motorsport brief. From February 1984 to its international competition debut in 1985, the motorsport Metro changed constantly and obviously.

Externally it grew in dimensions and sprouted some ugly, but effective, wings. These were mounted clear of the body to provide unobstructed airflow and,

together with the unturbocharged engine, were designed to provide the winning edge over ever more powerful opposition.

The 6R4 was 144 inches (3658 mm) long, compared to the production 1.3-litre Metro's 134 inches (3404 mm), and while the conventional Metro had a 60.1-inch (153 mm) girth, its rallying cousin had fattened to 73.2 inches (1859 mm). Similarly, the competition car used a track

whose width averaged at least 10 inches (254 mm) more than standard, while the wheelbase had grown from a factory-fresh 88.6 inches (2250 mm) to fractionally less than 95 inches (2413 mm).

Although the competition Metro used carbon fibre and lightweight aluminium in its body construction, the larger engine (three litres) and 4WD stystem made it considerably heavier than

the conventional production car: about 2156 lb (980 kg) versus less than 1692 lb (769 kg). Also increased were the wheel and tyre sizes: Dymag wheels, shod for the factory cars with Michelin tyres, measured up to 16 inches in diameter. Behind them were brakes as big as the production Metro's steel wheels: 12 inches (305 mm) in diameter.

Although early prototypes of the Metro 6R4 used the chopped Rover V8 test motors, the 90-degree V6 designed by the Motorsport department was sufficiently powerful and reliable to take the car to third place in its debut event, the November 1985 Lombard RAC Rally of Great Britain. The 2991 cc unit featured double overhead camshafts, twenty-four valves and a choice of power outputs.

For public sale, and the bulk of production, the Clubman tune allowed 250 bhp at 7000 rpm. The move from Lucas single-point injection to six-point and revision of the engine timing using replacement camshafts provided the International specification work cars with 410 bhp at a resounding 9000 rpm.

The absence of turbocharging gave the Metros an instant power response, free from the dreaded 'turbo lag' and mid-range pulling power was exceptional in both designs. The International developed 270 lb ft of torque at 6500 rpm (less pulling power as bhp escalated from 380 to 410 in factory trim); the Clubman was almost easy to drive on the road, having 225 lb ft at 4500 revs.

Unfortunately, the Lucas Micos

Below right The 6R4 was available with its V6 engine in two states of tune, 250 bhp for Clubmans events and a massive 410 bhp for International rallies

Far right Form has certainly been sacrificed for function with the 6R4, designed for speed its looks were irrelevant

electronically fuel-injected engine was prone to unreliability in its only World Championship season (1986) and the works team was inexperienced. That RAC Rally debut result was never bettered by team drivers Tony Pond, from the Isle of Man, and Cumbrian Malcolm Wilson.

As the company was keen to sell the 6R4 production run, many were used on the road, some of them re-trimmed and sound-proofed in an effort to beat the gnashing gear noises within.

The cabin is strictly for two, the engine hammering away like an unsilenced Porsche 911 and the unsynchronized Jack Knight five-speed gearbox clipping speedily, and noisily, through the ratios – that is if you can get the thing moving without stalling it on the competition clutch and flyweight flywheel. . . .

While a large MG-embossed Montego steering wheel guides this supremely responsive Metro in International trim – 0-60 mph (96 kph) takes some 3 seconds – the enormous brakes and all-wheel-drive grip emphasize that manufacturers are learning about new heights of performance in this supercar era of rallying.

MORGA

MMC 11

PLUS 8

MORGAN

There are two compelling reasons to buy a Morgan, or more particularly a V8 Morgan: its appealing appearance, and the unique style of fast motoring it provides. Seated in the car, your elbows crooked behind the three-spoke wheel, triple wipers and

copious instrumentation, you gaze over separated wings, bonnet vents and protuberant lights.

If the view ahead is one of unfurling country roads, you will enjoy to the full all the exhilaration to be had from applying the full weight of the unique 'roller ball' throttle. It is best if the day is dry

and the top down – for when the hood is erect, the creaks and groans are more noticeable – but we can safely say there is no motoring experience like that of driving a Morgan, and that must be why, in this age of 'Euro-boxes' and 'hot hatches', customers remain loyal to the marque.

A Morgan, any Morgan, is widely considered to be the epitome of the traditional British sports car, but that does not mean the cars from Malvern Link have not changed over the years. From 1950 to 1968, the Plus 4 model looked much the same as today's Plus 8, but the current V8 model has almost double the power of that offered in the '50s and '60s.

This bonus power has not been accompanied by a corresponding growth in weight, so shattering acceleration is guaranteed.

When the not unreasonable price of just £15 400 is taken into account, the Morgan could justifiably be described as one of the performance bargains of the '80s, but there is a lot more to sports motoring than simple acceleration statistics. There is one snag, however, a waiting list of more than five years. . . .

Morgan has been building three-wheelers and, later, sports cars at the same Worcestershire site since 1910. The name comes from the company owners,

generations of Morgans who have ensured that supply never outstrips demand, limiting production to fewer than twenty cars per week.

Some elements of the Plus 8's construction, such as the sliding-pillar front suspension, the ladder-type chassis in tubular steel and Z-section chassis frames, date back to the first four-wheeler Morgans of 1936. Incidentally, the hand-beaten panels are laid over an ash frame that is an equally long-standing ingredient in the Morgan recipe, but today it has the added refinement of Cuprinol preservative treatment.

The Plus 8 is a long-running model, even by Morgan standards – it has been produced

continuously since 1968. Even then, it took the end of the Triumph 100 bhp engine to force Morgan to look for an alternative motor, which came in the shape of Rover's alloy V8.

As today, capacity was 3528 cc, but the 90-degree eight has been considerably uprated from the original carburetted output of 155 bhp. American readers may remember the unit better as that used by Buick, while Australians will know that this lightweight eight also appeared in ill-starred local Leyland products of the '70s

Right Morgan have made some concessions to modern times, for example in the instruments but although they are analogue they do look slightly out of place

Below Alloy wheels, too, look a little incongruous but they are worthwhile for their reduced unsprung weight

as well as in imported Rovers.

The Plus 8 of the late '80s has gained Lucas electronic fuel injection and the production specification that Rover once used in its big hatchback Vitesse. That brings a smooth 190 bhp at 5280 rpm and an accessible 220 lb ft of torque – enough to fling the Morgan's 2022 lb (919 kg) to 60 mph (96 kph) in just 5.6 seconds.

Autocar figures reveal that this car falls into the same acceleration bracket as many fancier models, beating machinery such as Chevrolet's 1985 Corvette, Ferrari's Mondial V8, Lamborghini's Jalpa and smoother home-grown opposition from Lotus and TVR.

Naturally, the Morgan's upright lines – it is only 4 ft 4 in (1221 mm) tall – prevent it from achieving a high maximum speed, but, in a car of such uncompromising character, 126 mph (203 kph) is probably enough for all but dedicated racers. Incidentally, while the vented bonnet and flat windscreen epitomize Morgan appeal, the Plus 8's hand-built body has been offered clothed in alloy and steel panels.

Upon its debut, the Morgan Plus 8 featured an obstructive old Moss four-speed gearbox (also to be found in older Jaguars), but in the '70s Malvern Link adopted a later Rover four-speed, and in 1977 progressed to the present five-speed from the same source.

Changes have also been made to the steering. Originally it was of worm-and-nut type and had a very rapid response (2.4 turns lock-to-lock), but now it is the more conventional rack and pinion; that is almost as heavy in feel as before,

but is now slightly lower geared at more than three full turns of the wheel from lock-to-lock.

The suspension system does not always make its existence apparent over British bumps, but contrary to the malicious comments of rivals, we can confirm that Morgan does offer suspension front and rear! At the front is that venerable sliding pillar, which acts in conjunction with leaf and coil spring, plus telescopic dampers. At the rear is an equally traditional live axle, supported by leaf springs and lever-arm dampers of the type that

used to be commonplace.

Equipped with 6.5 x 15-inch alloy wheels and 205-section tyres the Morgan Plus 8 has impressive grip. In fact, its racing performances still shame many more modern designs, the combination of acceleration, braking and cornering prowess sufficient to take on legends such as the AC Cobra in circuit trim. In a hurry over wet and bumpy public roads it is much more difficult to keep the Plus 8 in a straight line for long, but owners forgive this and the heavy steering as insignificant

foibles in a car that has such character.

The Morgan's modest 2022 lb (919 kg) kerb weight means its brakes are not unduly stressed. Thus a mixed disc/drum brake layout is fitted, the front discs 11 inches in diameter and the rear drums spanning just 9 inches. Vacuum-servo assistance is used, but it still takes the kind of firm pressure that is needed to drive a Morgan fast to get the best from the Plus 8's stopping capabilities.

The hood looks more difficult to raise and lower than it proves in practice: the clips, arranged in a

. . . this car falls into the same acceleration bracket as many fancier models, beating machinery such as Chevrolet's Corvette, Ferrari's Mondial V8 and Lamborghini's Jalpa . . .

line across the top of the windscreen, are all cooperative and the Dzus fasteners securing the rear of the hood to the panelwork are also amenable to all but frozen fingers.

Never pass up the chance to passenger, or better still drive, a Morgan. It is the car for those who thrive on pure pleasure.

Above & right The timeless lines of the Morgan V8 Vitesse are executed in alloy, complementing the aluminium Rover V8 powerplant

MID 4

NISSAN

When the second-largest Japanese manufacturer speaks in production terms of a 180 mph-plus package of high-technology features and smooth styling, the traditional European supercar sources begin to wonder about the future – especially as Nissan and its two

editions of the Mid-4 were just one part of a wave of Japanese show cars that had production prospects.

By 1987 Nissan had developed a second generation of its high-tech wonder car – Mid 4-II. This car could have served the company in motor sports, but, Group S, in which it would compete, was scrapped. In any case, Nissan had apparently decided against manufacturing the twin-turbo flagship at a predicted limited-edition price equivalent to £33 300. Nissan thought the USA would be the primary market for such a supercar, and three pre-production Mid 4-IIs all conformed to Federal standards.

At the '87 Tokyo Show, from Suzuki's ingenious 1-litre RS-series upwards, the Japanese were obviously serious about cracking open yet another traditionally European preserve. Apart from its technically interesting gas-turbine prototype, Toyota's most imposing show machine was the slippery

> *... the potential for an unusually responsive sports coupé at half the price of some Ferraris ... this will not be the last we hear of Nissan's performance aspirations*

and mobile FXV-II, powered by a production-scheduled 32-valve V8 of 3.8 litres and 235 bhp.

While the Europeans wondered if features such as four-wheel steering (4WS) were a gimmick, Hondas, Mazdas, Nissans and Mitsubishis poured from the 1987-8 production lines, their rear wheels helping those in front with the steering chores. Nissan had even transferred its 4WS research into saloon-car racing, and Mitsubishi looked set to tackle World Championship rallying equipped with a production-based saloon that packaged 4WS *and* 4WD. Meanwhile American, German and British engineers had to be content with examining 4WS at the prototype stage. . . . The Japanese have left their copying days far behind.

The Mid 4 tag denotes that the car is mid-engined and has 4WD, 4WS, four valves for each cylinder and four overhead camshafts.

That 230 bhp show car was aimed at the European market to show the engineering standards that Nissan could attain. Thus in September 1986, it was debuted in Frankfurt, right inside Europe's largest and most technically aware market: Germany.

Before the 1987 Tokyo Motor Show, Nissan allowed a small number of journalists to drive the Mid 4-II, and it was obvious that the Japanese giant was still pondering the merits of a prestige production two-seater.

Externally the later Mid 4-II bore a family likeness to the 1986

Above left The Mid 4-II's engine is a development of the V6 used in the latest of the Z cars, the 300ZX Turbo, equipped with twin-overhead cams per cylinder bank and twin turbos

Left The engine hatch treatment would clearly be revised before production . . .

NISSAN

NISSAN

mi04

original, but obvious modifications included a cleaner rear end design, in which the exhausts were separated rather than clustered, and a power bulge atop the rear engine deck-lid.

Dimensionally, the Mid 4-II had grown wider and longer. The wheelbase had been increased by more than 4 inches to 100 inches (2540 mm) in total, a move in keeping with the extended cockpit. Overall length was increased by almost 6 inches to 169 inches (4293 mm), while the width was substantial at 73 inches (1854 mm), reflecting the use of a side water radiator instead of the original car's front-mounted cooling.

Body height was much the same as in the first Mid 4 and rather greater than current exotica from Lamborghini and Ferrari, at 47 inches (1194 mm). The effect was of a sports racing front end allied to the rear end glass and chunkiness of an Italian supercar – not the happiest of marriages.

The mechanical specification had altered considerably. The mid-mounted V6, which is of Nissan 300ZX parentage, had been turned around from a transverse position to run in line at the rear. The 60-degree unit was equipped with Nissan's advanced ceramic-rotor twin turbos, whereas the first Mid 4 had lacked turbocharging. The newer unit ran a lower compression (8.5:1) and retained double overhead camshafts (dohc) for each cylinder bank of the 3-litre unit.

Maximum quoted horsepower had risen by 100 bhp to compensate for similarly inflated

Right The rear is not the Mid 4-II's best feature; side views **(far right)** show it off to far better advantage

Below The interior is everything any self-respecting supercar would be proud of, a world away from Japanese production designs

body weight of 3080 lb (1400 kg). Instead of 230 bhp, Nissan reported 330 bhp at 6800 rpm and said that the 3200 rpm torque peak brought 277 lb ft of pulling power.

Performance of the new-technology Nissan was in the upper echelons of the present supercar breed. The company claimed a 186 mph maximum along with an unfrenzied 5 seconds from 0 to 62 mph, the 4WD system reducing the tyre pyrotechnics usually caused by a fast getaway.

The chassis was improved, too. Strut front suspension was dispensed with in favour of double wishbones, while the rear suspension highlighted a limited implementation of 4WS principles that restricted toe-in and out movement to some 2 degrees, a fraction of that allowed in current Mazda and Honda 4WS. The 4WD system deployed familiar epicyclic gearing components to split the power thirty-five per cent front and sixty-five per cent rear. The kerb weight of more than 3000 lb (1364 kg) was also deliberately split unevenly – forty per cent over the front wheels and sixty per cent over the rear, figures which Nissan wanted to retain in this mid-engined car, for handling reasons.

Assisting the slip-free

application of power were three Ferguson-patent viscous couplings in central, aft and front differentials. Such efficient power allocation allowed Nissan to use comparatively modest – by supercar standards – alloy wheel rim widths: 7.5-inch front and 8-inch rear. Some early demonstrators came equipped with Bridgestone's reputable RE71 performance tyres (the same company supplied rubber for Porsche's fabled 959). These tyres were a mixture of low-profile 50- and 55-series, measuring up to 235 mm in width.

The prototype interior was sombrely trimmed in black and appeared to have everything in the way of seat location, ergonomic switchgear and clear instrumentation (via black and white dials) that a serious driver would need. The speedometer indicated to 180 mph (288 kph) and the tachometer was red-lined just beyond 7000 rpm. The door sills were not exceptionally wide, in Ferrari Testarossa or Lamborghini style, but the overall effect was that this was a very serious attempt at realistic production engineering.

In action, the Mid 4-II was not quite so convincing, exhibiting some straight-line instability and marked down to a 168 mph (269 kph) maximum by company personnel. However, the potential for an unusually grippy and responsive sports coupé at half the price of some Ferraris and Porsches is obviously present. We can be sure this will not be the last we hear of Nissan's upwardly mobile performance aspirations.

SOLO
PANTHER

Master of the motor show art of building up public excitement for future production plans, Panther Cars is as individualistic as more typically British concerns such as Morgan and Caterham Cars. For nearly ten years it existed on the '30s look of machines such as the Kallister two-seater, but the recent Solo designs have firmly broken that mould and established the company's identity in the field of mid-engined motoring.

The first Solo design promised the cheaper end of the two-seater market a Ford Escort-engined bargain. That was at the

Birmingham International Motor Show of October 1984, but despite an appearance that had potential customers queuing the car has yet to be produced.

Solo 2 which has followed that original, also has sharp styling by consultants John Heffernan and Ken Greenley, but a much more sophisticated design lies beneath its composite-construction panelwork than in the original.

Planned for production in April 1989 (at least ten running examples will have been completed by the end of 1988 for international certification in respect of emissions and crash testing), Solo 2 will have a price

tag of £30 000. Only thus can it avoid the commercial suicide entailed by taking on mass manufacturers when handicapped by specialist overheads and low volumes.

It is thought that Panther may one day build the cheaper mark 1 Solo, which was aimed at the market segment now dominated by Toyota's MR2. Panther would then also have to compete with the Lotus 'Elan'/ M100, since from 1989 Lotus will be challenging the cheaper Japanese sports choices.

Solo 2's aspirations in the higher price bracket are based on a package of advanced technical features not seen elsewhere when

the car was first shown (Frankfurt, September 1987). It was the first car to combine the Ford-Cosworth sixteen-valve turbo engine with the sophisticated four-wheel-drive (4WD) system whose main elements had already been seen in the Sierra and Scorpio 4x4 saloons.

Yet it was the construction of the 2200 lb (1000 kg) car that broke the most new ground, for Panther had drawn on the composite technology of formula car racing, successfully approaching March Engineering's Comtec division for a production design.

The result was a two-plus-two body with front luggage

compartment that was built in a combination of epoxy resin, aluminium honeycomb and interwoven carbon and glass

fibres. That high-tech concoction is bonded to a rather more traditional central chassis, made from welded steel sheets. Multi-tube outriggers extend front and rear to locate engine and transmission units.

The 171-inch (4343 mm) long, two-door car (the back section hinges to allow access to the north-south four-cylinder engine) spent a lot of time, at the one-third model stage, in March's Buckinghamshire wind tunnel. The designers could not evolve an attractive shape that would generate the necessary stabilizing downforces, except by incorporating the rather large rear wing, ridged front spoiler and deep air intake ducts ahead of the rear wheels.

The declared aerodynamic drag coefficient is 0.33, which is not exceptional when you consider that Renault is already producing

an Alpine GTA with 0.29. Indeed, there are plenty of production saloons recording a sleek 0.30 factor, and they do not have the aerodynamic and handling advantage of bodywork just 46 inches (1168 mm) in height.

The running gear centres on all-independent wishbone suspension, the front units featuring MacPherson struts as well. Wheel and tyre selections are not the most adventurous seen in modern motoring – attractive 6J x 15-inch cast alloy rims support Goodyear NCT Eagles of 195/50-VR section. Despite this modest (by the Solo's 150 mph standards) tyre width, the Panther Solo 2 reportedly exceeded 0.9g in preliminary cornering trials.

No power assistance was thought necessary for the rack-and-pinion steering, but the four-wheel disc brakes – ventilated at the front only – are supported by

Above The advanced composites of the Solo's body are formed to suitably futuristic forms

Right Your eyes are not deceiving you, the Cosworth twin-cam is mounted longitudinally at an angle to accommodate the four-wheel drivetrain

Right In common with a host of other supercars, the Solo's interior is characterized by its massive central spine

Below Taking a leaf out of the Japanese manufacturers' book, advertising all the car's assets on the outside

Below right Beneath the lockable alloy wheels can be seen the appropriately massive discs necessary to haul the Solo down from its projected 150 mph top speed

the German Ate electronic anti-lock layout of the type seen on SAAB and Ford saloons.

Conceived for left- or right-hand-drive production, Solo 2 employs a Common Market emissions standard engine, but, alternatively, a Ford V6 could be installed. The Ford-Cosworth unit retains conventional Sierra RS Cosworth power trim – 0.7-0.9 bar boost from the Garrett AiResearch

The all-wheel-drive system adds a new dimension . . . the extra grip conferred by such a system . . . allow Panther to claim 0-60 mph will occupy no more than 5.7 seconds

turbocharger releases an official 204 bhp at 6000 rpm.

Installed at a slight angle in that rear bay to accommodate the 4WD components in its vicinity, the double-overhead-camshaft unit also provides more than 200 lb ft of torque – pulling power that is delivered progressively with the help of Weber-Marelli electronic management.

The 4WD system is not exactly as employed by Ford, but Ferguson patents still apply to the central and rear differential viscous couplings to limit slippage. Like the Cosworth Sierras, Solo 2 employs a Borg Warner T5 gearbox to provide a quintet of ratios. The transfer box to split power forward and aft at a ratio of thirty-four per cent front and sixty-six per cent rear is of Panther design, albeit with a large initial input from Ford-trained sources.

The all-wheel-drive system adds a new dimension to mid-engined motoring. The extra grip conferred by such a system and the car's light kerb weight allow Panther to claim that 0-60 mph (96 kph) will occupy no more than 5.7 seconds. The company, in advance of production models being available for independent testing, was also confident that the maximum speed would be 150 mph (240 kph). It seems realistic to expect at least 21-24 mpg in daily use. By the close of 1987 nearly

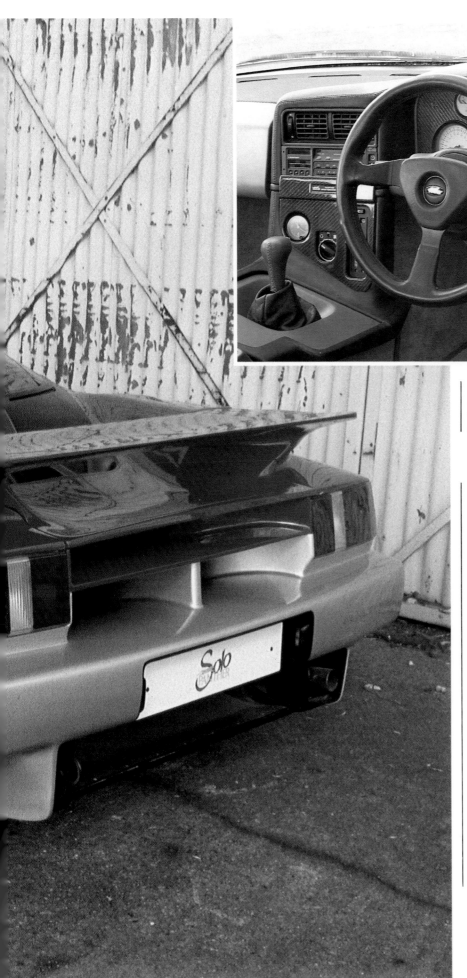

Left Function or style? Panther argue the Solo is a perfect blend

Above The central tachometer totally dominates the dial-packed facia

one hundred people had paid deposits of £500 each to become Panther Solo 2 owners when production starts. Prominent inside the prototype car are the large dials with their stylish white backgrounds, the three-spoke sports steering wheel and leather trim added to an interior that is closest in concept to that of a Lotus.

Writing in advance of full production it is difficult to portray the Solo 2 that customers will receive, but have no doubt that the Panther Solo 2 will have its own unique character.

Panther customers in 1989 will receive the bulk of their supplies from a new Panther factory at Harlow in Essex, rather than the Brooklands premises.

205 T16

PEUGEOT

The most successful design to emerge from rallying's highest-powered World Championship era (Group B, 1982-6) was the chunky Peugeot 205 T16. Its radical specification enabled it to conquer two World Championships, win the 1987 Paris-Dakar and father

the company's 1988 Paris-Dakar contender, the 405 T16.

Until Peugeot arrived on the World Championship scene with its purpose-built 'rally-racer', Audi had the series wrapped up. The German team had introduced turbocharging and four-wheel drive (4WD), setting a new

standard of grip on slippery surfaces.

However, Peugeot had spotted the weak link in those awesomely powerful five-cylinder Audis: at the end of the day, they were still just converted road cars, retaining a front-engined layout and fifty-fifty power distribution to front

and rear wheels. Peugeot reasoned that it could do the job better, over a wider variety of surfaces (Audi had never been very successful on dry tarmac), using a car created specifically for competition. The clever commercial touch was to make the T16 ('T' for turbocharged, '16'

Right Outrageous wing apart, the T16 looks like a conventional road-going 205 in smart livery but it's a complete illusion, the car being a mid-engined device with a centre monocoque and unstressed body panels

Far right The all-alloy 16-valve twin-cam is turbocharged and intercooled to produce 200 bhp at 6750 rpm

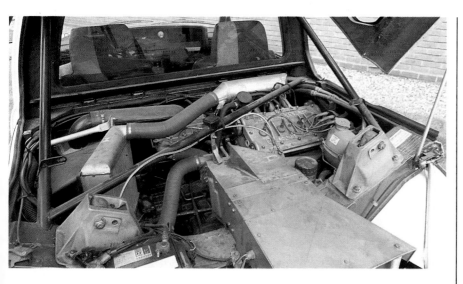

for the number of valves employed in its four cylinders) appear similar to its new 205 front-drive hatchback. Any competition success, and there would be four World Championship titles in 1985-6, would add to the kudos of owning a new 205.

To qualify for World Championship rallying in the Group B 'supercar' category, Peugeot had to build 200 T16s, all equipped with the basics of the 'works' cars; these were offered at more than £25 000 each. Subsequently, further batches of twenty were offered to the public in 'Evolution' specification (E1 and E2) which had even greater power and aerodynamics. All were in left-hand drive.

The 205 T16 *version client* was detailed for the world in February 1984 and displayed publicly at that year's Geneva motor show. Working from design principles established in January 1982 under the leadership of Peugeot Talbot Sport director (and former rally co-driver) Jean Todt, Peugeot engineers created a sophisticated winner.

Sporting mid-engined layout and 4WD, this car bounded along, its electronically fuel-injected turbo motor providing 320 to 350 bhp from the start of its competitive life, which was in Corsica in May 1984. It led its first event and in the hands of Finland's Ari Vatanen, quickly became a victor; fellow Finns Juha Kankkunen and Timo Salonen won their World Championship titles in later Peugeot Sport T16s.

No rival has followed Peugeot in placing the engine across the middle of the car, rather than in-line. It makes for an exceptionally compact competitor, one that measures just 150.4 inches (3820 mm) long.

Comparative width and wheelbase figures are generous in the pursuit of maximum roadholding and a stable ride. The customer version is just under 67 inches (1700 mm) wide and stands on a 100-inch (2540 mm) wheelbase. Such statistics represent significant increases over the standard 205 GTi, which is 4.7 inches (119 mm) shorter, 5 inches (127 mm) slimmer, and whose wheelbase is 4.7 inches (119 mm) smaller.

The car comprises a central, two-seater monocoque in pressed steel with a front extension of mixed panel and box-section steel construction and a tubular rear frame to carry the engine and transmission. The cars for public consumption have steel roof or polyester panelwork, but lightweight panels were a feature only of the further-developed Evolution versions. In road trim, the T16 weighs 2519 lb (1149 kg), but the more powerful competition cars tip the scales at around 2134 lb (970 kg).

The 4WD system is sophisticated; epicyclic gears apportion power on a split that can be varied from seventy-five per cent front/twenty-five per cent rear to forty-five/fifty-five per cent front/rear. Peugeot learned that the latter ratio was best for slippery conditions, while over more grippy surfaces, less power should be fed to the front wheels.

Additional transmission features needed in a car that was going to be rallying over arctic ice and Safari sands, included British Ferguson-patented viscous couplings to limit the slip of the central differential and, for the most powerful rally versions, the front and rear differentials, too. In customer T16s the central viscous coupling is supported by a conventional ZF rear limited-slip differential.

A six-speed gearbox was debuted for competition in April 1986, by which time the 205 T16 had established that it was the standard by which other Group B supercars could be judged, harnessing close to 500 bhp in its later form, and possessing outstanding traction and handling.

The suspension system is based on double wishbones plus a combined coil spring/damper at each corner, and a wide choice of anti-roll bars to fit front and rear. One of the few weaknesses discovered during the car's competitive life was its appetite for dampers over rough ground; it could have done with the double-damper layout found on some rivals.

At first, the steering of both road and rally cars was unassisted, but the more powerful E2 rally cars were equipped with power steering, which had become a necessity in such powerful machines.

Instead of the 130 bhp to be found in the most powerful 1.9 GTis, the T16's similarly all-aluminium construction (the block is of Peugeot-Citroën production origin) boasts 70 extra horsepower with its double-overhead-camshafts and sixteen valves. That extra power demands the use of forged steel for both crankshaft and connecting rods. In road trim, with force-feeding from a KKK turbocharger and intercooler, that 200 bhp comes at 6750 rpm, with a 6.5:1 compression ratio.

But that is nothing alongside the factory-entered rally cars. A 1775 cc engine (instead of 1600), with a larger turbocharger and many more power-based modifications yielded 350 bhp at 8000 rpm. Even that considerable power – enough to flick the little Pug from rest to 100 mph (160 kph) in less than 10 seconds –

Below left Ari Vatanen's T16 storms across the desert in the '88 Paris-Dakar; his chances of victory vanished when his car was stolen . . .

Left The drilled pedals and Turbo 16 label on the steering wheel are all that give the game away

. . . an even larger Garrett turbocharger of Grand Prix racing dimensions was employed to coax a minimum of 435 bhp from the 1.8 litres . . .

was augmented during the course of 1984.

Then an even larger Garrett turbocharger, of Grand Prix racing dimensions, was employed to coax a minimum of 435 bhp from the 1.8 litres. This enhanced the Evolution 2 model's accelerative powers to the point where it would scamper to 60 mph (96 kph) in 3.3 seconds and scorch onwards, up to 100 mph (160 kph) in 8 seconds. It would rush to 110 mph (176 kph) in the same time as the earlier model

took to reach 100 mph (160 kph): around 9.5 seconds.

As competition or road cars, the T16s were and are impressive. On the road, the 200 bhp version dislikes providing pulling power much below 4000 rpm, so you have to work hard to reach 60 mph (96 kph) in 7.8 seconds, or its 130 mph (208 kph) maximum. However, its large diameter wheels and excellent chassis provide an accurate taste of the 'real rally car's' phenomenal agility and exhilarating pace.

911 SPEEDSTER

PORSCHE

Although Porsche chairman Peter Schutz departed the company abruptly in late 1987, the legacy of his determination to breathe new life into the timeless 911 continues to produce new derivatives. For it was Schutz who insisted that the flat-six-cylinder

engine still had plenty of room for development, and he who backed the production of the fastest and most sophisticated Porsche to date: the four-wheel-drive, twin-turbo 959 of 1987.

The Speedster reviewed on these pages represents an attempt to revive older Porsche glories –

resurrecting a badge and a style made famous between 1954 and '59 on a four-cylinder 356 base.

While the 190 mph (304 kph) transformation of 911 into 959 dazzled onlookers, Peter Schutz was ensuring that the technical lessons learned were passed along in a more affordable form to

provide four-wheel-drive 911 derivatives for the 1990s. But the 911 Speedster, like the Club Sport 911, represents a production foray into reviving the old 911 virtues of light weight and amateur motorsport success.

The Speedster was debuted at the September 1987 Frankfurt

Show, but it was to be about a year before it was offered to the public. And its production, at the Porsche factory in the Stuttgart suburb of Zuffenhausen, was provisionally limited to fewer than ten Speedsters a day.

The Speedster has brought a new guise to conventional 911 running gear. Special features include an abbreviated and raked windscreen and a startling pvc 'hunchback' to streamline the space behind the front seats and above the air grilles of the rear engine cover.

The decision to resurrect the Speedster name came in 1982, when Schutz was told by his all-important American dealers (who took more than sixty per cent of

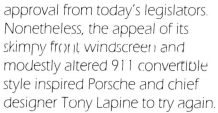

Below From the top of the wings down, the Porsche Speedster looks like any of the other famous cars in the 911 family. From there up, however, it is different with a steeper-raked windscreen and a solid tonneau

Porsche production) that the newly wealthy 'Yuppies' would see such a car as the ultimate status symbol. A prototype was completed during the spring of 1983, but it lacked any of the detailing needed to obtain approval from today's legislators. Nonetheless, the appeal of its skimpy front windscreen and modestly altered 911 convertible style inspired Porsche and chief designer Tony Lapine to try again.

The result was a dual-purpose approach. Taking an open 911 as the basic starting point, Porsche would provide equipment alternatives to convert that car into an American national racer. The Club Sport specification would not be road legal, featuring a windscreen so severely abbreviated that to provide wipers would be impracticable, and only one usable seat.

Transforming the Speedster into Club Sport trim requires two knowledgeable operators, because the larger windscreen is securely screwed to the body; also, the wipers have to be removed and the passenger seat unbolted.

The trickiest task we could see at the car's German unveiling was fitting the sea-shell cover in place of the plain Speedster's soft top; that's because the Sport panel is uncharacteristically heavy and is secured via those redundant front wiper drive spindles. Once fitted the Club Sport shell envelops the cockpit so completely that the driver's priority problem is how to gain access without permanently damaging his contorted anatomy.

Driving the Speedster is a windswept, but exciting, experience. The skimpily framed windscreen and low driving position conspire to give a totally fresh feel to the car. In fact it is almost like riding a motorcycle, such is the blasting from the wind.

S · JN 7392

Driving the Speedster is a windswept, but exciting, experience. The skimpily framed windscreen and a low driving position conspire to give a totally fresh feel to the car

Below & right
From a closed coupé, the 911 Porsche has evolved firstly as a Targa, where a roof panel lifts off and stows in the car, to a full Convertible and now to a roadster

Porsche's use of front tyres narrower than those of the rear, plus a torsion bar front suspension that has been developed to cope with low-profile tyres, means the 911 now has considerably higher cornering limits than it had upon its production debut.

Over the years, Porsche has managed to delay the onset of the tail-out oversteer that marks the limit of cornering power in any rear-engined car, but the 911 will still bite back if cornered too ambitiously. The compensation, however, is accelerative traction in the four-wheel-drive class, a marvellously alert feel to the steering and powerful disc brakes. But, it is that supreme air-cooled six-cylinder engine that sells so many of these cars. No other power unit has won such diverse

motor-sporting awards, from Le Mans to Monte Carlo, and given such customer satisfaction.

In Britain we are accustomed to Porsche 911s without exhaust-emission controls, producing 231 bhp from their 3.2-litre engines – impulsion released to the glorious tune of 5900 rpm. However, it is likely that the Speedster – which might well be revamped, since initial public reaction to the styling was far from universally welcoming – will stick with the catalytic-convertor version of the famous flat-six. Thus equipped, it produces no more than 217 bhp at 5700 rpm and peak torque would drop from 210 lb ft to 195 lb ft, both at 4800 rpm.

Performance will be slightly boosted over the standard car by the modest reduction in kerb weight, but will hover around 6 seconds for 0-62 mph (100 kph) and a draughty maximum of less than 149 mph (238 kph). Such figures contrast with that 231-horsepower, UK-spec 911's ability to exceed 150 mph

(240 kph) and rush from 0-60 mph (96 kph) in less than 5.5 seconds. Fuel consumption should remain better than 20 mpg.

By the time the Speedster was scheduled for manufacture, Porsche had been forced to face some unpleasant managerial decisions. In the USA and UK, Porsche prices had escalated in unison with the strength of the Deutschmark and demand had nose-dived accordingly. This financial factor, along with concerted sales opposition from the Japanese in the cheaper sports sector (which hit production of four-cylinder Porsches severely) led to Porsche reassessing its position and one of the earliest reactions was to replace Peter Schutz as chairman with the finance-orientated Heinz Branitzki, who had previously been his deputy.

The effect upon the 911 Speedster remained to be seen, but, whatever happened, Porsche's approach to fresh-air motoring in the late 1980s was unique.

ALPINE GTA

RENAULT

A direct challenge to Porsche's 911, but constructed by methods more familiar at Lotus, the rear-engined Renault Alpines have yet to catch the performance purchaser's imagination. This is surprising considering the turbocharged version's expensive European

racing programme, and the fact that, in standard production trim, the Alpine can exceed 150 mph (241 kph). Thus far it has been a story of great potential and dramatically effective styling that has yet to be fully appreciated.

In Britain the two-plus-two coupés from the Renault-owned Alpine works in the port of Dieppe do not carry the Alpine badge that was made famous by generations of rapid rally cars. Competition Alpines were based upon Renault running gear and won at Le Mans and Monte Carlo, but in the UK the Alpine badge is registered with another manufacturer, so the coupés must be known as Renault GTA V6 and V6 Turbo respectively.

Both models, the turbocharged version costing more than £25 000 and its fuel-injected cousin fully £5000 less, are sold in Britain. Right-hand drive supplies are limited to hundreds and they remain a comparatively rare sight in Britain.

For the most part the two models share specifications, but

what differences there are lie in that back engine bay. In both cases the basic V6 power unit and five-speed transaxle serve the Renault 25's front-wheel-drive layout. The multiple-carburettor V6 measures 2.8 litres and develops an unstressed 160 bhp.

The GTA Turbo has an entirely new crankshaft, of fundamentally different balance characteristics, that provides 2.5 litres. Complete with a larger intercooler and other detail modifications over the Renault 25 saloon, this Renix electronically fuel-injected V6 yields 200 bhp, or 185 for an export emission-controlled catalytic-convertor derivative.

Judged simply as modified production engines, these Renault V6s provide good, though not exceptional, power for their capacity. What makes the GTA coupés so fast in a straight line is remarkably aerodynamic bodywork, assisted in cutting cleanly through the air by a squat 47-inch (1194 mm) overall height. The result is one of the lowest quoted aerodynamic drag factors in production (0.28) for the 160 bhp GTA. Wider wheels and tyres fitted as standard to the Turbo (and optionally available on the less powerful car) fill more of the 170.5-inch (4331 mm)-long hull, but still allow an outstanding 0.30 Cd.

Lotus's Excel and Esprit models are built by the same broad principles – external glassfibre moulds over a steel backbone chassis – but the detail differences in the production process are considerable: for example, the Renault does not have the galvanized chassis of the Lotus.

Rear-engined cars, by their very nature, suffer instability in hard cornering or motorway crosswinds, but advantages include traction almost in the 4WD class and steering so light that it requires no artificial sweeteners, such as power assistance. This is quite an achievement on the Turbo GTA, for it has 6-inch-wide front wheels and massive 8.5-inch-wide rears – a lot of rubber to handle with such ease at parking speeds.

Renault have equipped the GTA with every proven handling

. . . every proven handling and braking device – the double wish-bone suspension and four-wheel vented disc braking system permit exceptional safety . . .

and braking device – the double-wishbone suspension and four-wheel vented disc braking system permit exceptional safety even when driven hard on the track. Complemented by immense low-profile tyres on the turbo model, there is no shortage of grip.

On a more mundane level the

Left Renault have managed to achieve an extremely efficient aerodynamic shape (Cd is an excellent 0.28) with equally attractive sleek lines

Far left In turbocharged form the GTA's fuel-injected V6 displaces 2.5 litres and produces 200 bhp

Below The interior is typically French; the eagle eyed will spot many components common to the Renault 25 saloon

GTAs offer plenty in the way of electrical assistance: little luxuries such as remote-controlled central locking, electric window- and door-opening and the Renault-Philips 4 x 20W stereo system are all standard. Weighing in at more than 2500 lb (1136 kg), these cars are not particularly light, but you can see where the temptation to produce a 'road racer' has been avoided in the high standards of paint and body finish.

Although plenty of instrumentation is provided and the shaped leather rim steering wheel provides the authentic feel of a low-slung sports two-plus-two, it is within the cabin that many have found the GTA uninspired. To keep prices below those of Porsche (but in much the same region as Lotus), Renault and Alpine agreed to use as much mass-production hardware as possible. The result is a cabin that abounds with familiar, mass-production dials and controls that do not look entirely at home in their new environment. Some may also be put off by the pedals which sprout from the floor.

The turbocharged model is most impressive in action, but that does not mean it is noisy in the traditional sports car sense – in fact, it starts and runs with all the modest demeanour you would expect of a large saloon. But when the Garrett turbocharger has its interest sufficiently engaged by engine revs beyond a mere 2500, this proves itself a truly fast car. Flat out to surpass the noisier 5750 rpm power peak, the Turbo will provide 0-60 mph (96 kph) in less than 6.5 seconds. It runs to nearly

Left Proof that it's possible to achieve a perfect mirror finish in composite materials

Above The French number plate tells a story; there's few GTAs around outside France

90 mph (145 kph) in the third of its five gears; an ignition cut-out protects the V6 from damage beyond 6100 revs.

The non-turbocharged GTA takes about a second longer to sprint to 60 mph (96 kph), but is less than 10 mph (16 kph) slower than the GTA Turbo's official 155 mph (249 kph) maximum. This is because its superior aerodynamic drag factor helps offset the deficiency of 40 bhp.

Steering and brakes on both models are prompt and precise. However, even Renault's considerable resources could not overcome the meandering progress of a rear-engined car under the influence of modest motorway crosswinds; this disconcerting characteristic takes some getting used to.

The stunning body style does incur windscreen reflections, but this is a small penalty to pay for the benefits to aerodynamics of a steeply raked screen. Interior comfort is above average since the V6's distance from the cabin dulls its already modest exhaust to a limousine's hum at high cruising speeds.

Overall the Renault GTA looks as though it stepped upon planet Earth ahead of its time, and it may well be that in the future, Renault-Alpine will be rewarded with many more customers as potential buyers learn of its efficiently enjoyable existence . . . and its competitive price.

HF 2000

TRANSFORMER

The rally stages of the early 1970s were transformed by Lancia in 1971. Up until then, rally winners had all been easily connected with road cars, like the Escorts and Minis of this world. Lancia decided that if you needed a very special tool to be successful in World Championship car racing, it would be sensible to have a specialist machine with which to contend World

Championships off-road.

In 1970, the Italian styling specialists Bertone produced a striking design study using a Lancia V4 engine. The car was called the Stratos, but it was a completely different beast which appeared the following year bearing the same name. The rallying Lancia Stratos came, saw and conquered and took the world title from 1974 to 1976.

The Stratos could never have

Above The Transformer's body is an exact replica of the classic Stratos, as indeed it should be with the moulds taken from the genuine article

Left The Lancia Beta powertrain fits neatly between the Transformer's extremely robust chassis members where there's room for the likes of a Renault V6

been described as beautiful, but there was no denying its purpose as it headed many rallies in the hands of pilots like Sandro Munari and Markku Alèn. The heart of the Lancia was its engine, that beautiful V6 Dino Ferrari unit that growled its power through the forests in a way in which no other car had done before or has done since. This delightful power plant had been developed from an F2 motor and found fame in the pretty Ferrari Dino 246GT and it was ideal for the Lancia.

The Transformer is just about indistinguishable from the Stratos, which is no surprise really, since its body moulds were taken from a Lancia original. How did the quartet of enthusiasts at

Above The Stratos shape dates back nearly two decades but it's still dramatically striking – the 'Q' number plate denotes that it is a kit

Above right The makers have wisely resisted the temptation to make the interior more luxurious than the original

Q334 JKO

Transformer in East Sussex get an original? Quite easy really: they offered to restore a Stratos in return for taking some moulds from its curvaceous body. They weren't content with that, however, and when the first body popped out of the mould they spent ages sanding it down and honing it until it was perfect. The original, you see, was full of blemishes. That should be seen as no criticism of Lancia craftsmanship, because the cars were built purely as competition tools and not as potential *concours* winners.

The construction is faithful to the Lancia, too, except that where the Lancia has a steel central body section with glassfibre nose and rear the Transformer is all constructed in glass-reinforced plastic. The chassis are identical, with a central tubular frame doubling as a sturdy roll cage. There are subframes front and rear to take the essentially Fiat/Lancia-sourced suspension components, while the easiest power unit/transmission to accommodate is the Fiat/Lancia twin-cam unit. These come in capacities from 1600 to 2000 cc and can even be supercharged, if you opt for one of the Volumex units fitted to the

Lancia Beta Coupé and HPE versions. The whole motor and gearbox assembly mounts straight on to the engine cage, along with the modified suspension.

Tuning kits are readily available for the Italian four-cylinder engines, but there have been Transformers built with more exotic power units. A couple have had Renault V6 power, while one lucky owner managed to acquire a Ferrari 246 Dino engine to make a real Stratos replica.

Keen to make the Transformer HF2000 resemble the Lancia as closely as possible, but also keen to improve on the original wherever possible, Messrs Artus, Hawkridge, Morris and Cruickshank set about making their car a little more practical than the Italian. The rear bulkhead is further back than on the original, allowing more cockpit space, while the seats are lower, too, just so that drivers larger than compact rally stars may be accommodated!

Inside, too, the Transformer is hard to distinguish from a Stratos, with its small, neat group of instruments nestling together in a brushed-aluminium nacelle and the bare minimum of luxury. Indeed, a heater is very much an optional extra! Again the original was a car built to do a job, and the Transformer is built to mirror the original.

The biggest difference between driving the two virtually identical cars (albeit ones with around sixteen years between them) is that the HF2000 was designed around much more modern and capable tyres than those that the Stratos had available to it, which were rather soft 70-section items. The HF sits on Pirelli P7 low-profile covers which give much more precise steering and better grip at the cost of a firmer ride. Slipping from one car to another would convince anyone that the two cars are identical – until their engines are fired up. The Transformer demonstrator is fitted with a tuned 180 bhp Lancia twin-cam motor which, although providing excellent performance, is rather rough and unwilling. The Stratos, by comparison, revs sweetly and spins its rev-counter needle eagerly around the dial at the merest hint of right foot on the throttle pedal. The Transformer's gearchange is firm and a little vague, but that on the Lancia is like stirring a very thin soup: the lever flops about all over the place and finding any gear is something of a lottery; in the Ferrari Dino, its lever was guided by a chrome-plated gate.

Stratoses (Strati?) were renowned for their nervous handling, caused by a very short wheelbase which itself gave the benefit of sharp handling reactions and incredible manoeuvrability. However, hair-trigger responses are fine for driving at ten-tenths in a forest, but not much use when you are driving swiftly on ordinary roads and it starts to rain. It is here that the Transformer is a leap ahead of the Lancia: it is more forgiving, courtesy of its more up-to-date tyres and the fact that, because its tyres are of much lower profile, the whole car sits lower.

The Transformer's steering is heavier, although this can easily be rectified with the all-adjustable suspension. It makes the car feel a lot more stable, too, which is important when the car is travelling across unknown roads quickly. Make no mistake, the Transformer is a very quick car, weighing less than a ton and packing around 180 bhp. Its handling is as faultless as one would expect from a mid-engined thoroughbred, with prodigious grip to match, and the whole car snorts along the road like the Groundhogs used to in the television adverts for Dunlop tyres; indeed, from some angles, the Transformer resembles one of those cuddly, wheeled beasts.

Lancia in Italy approve of the Transformer, taking the sensible view of 'replicars' that if it is well made, then it won't harm the image of their original, and Lancia can't deny that the Sussex stunner is anything but a very faithful copy. At the end of 1987, Transformer had a demonstrator which mirrored the Stratos even more. It

Right Lancia dials provide all the information you could possibly require. Note the exposed chassis members

Below Resplendent in its Alitalia colours, the Transformer is even more evocative of the original

Bottom The Alitalia car's massive Pirelli P7s give more grip than the original car

was fitted with a bank of four spotlights on its nose and finished in the red, white and green livery of the Alitalia airline which sponsored the factory rally cars for a time. However good it looked, though, it can never compare with the real thing – unless it has that glorious Ferrari engine nestling in its bay. This not only gave the Lancia Stratoses the right speed, but came up with the right noises too!

TRESER SPORTS

TRESER

Berlin-based Walter Treser is a man with an interesting history. Although middle-aged, he has built upon experiences gained from his time at Audi Volkswagen, to come up with a youthful mid-engined sports car of his own. The Treser roadster and coupé two-seaters were drawn up in much their present form by late 1983 and were

scheduled to go on public sale from a factory in northern Berlin in summer 1988.

Costing the equivalent of £30 000 in uniquely convertible roadster form, or £1667 less with fixed head coupé bodywork, the Treser was due to be powered by a catalytic-convertor version of VW's sixteen-valve Golf engine. However, the stubby 159.3-inch (4045 mm) machine in its attractive glassfibre body looks capable of coping with a good deal more power.

Interesting bodywork features include a unique swinging 'flip-top' hard top for the roadster, integrated spoilers that do not protrude at either front or rear, and pronounced 'ground-effect' tunnelling within a smooth underbody finish. Conscientious and clever management of air has promoted outstanding handling, and harnessed principles that Grand Prix racing has proved effective in boosting cornering grip.

Walter Treser was a respected figure in the fields of engineering and competition long before he established his own business in the early 1980s. Educated in Hamburg, Herr Treser worked for Daimler-Benz and in the tyre industry, before joining Audi as an engineer. He was effectively the 'father' of the revolutionary Audi quattro coupé, being the project engineer for that 1980 Geneva Show debutant.

When the quattro went World Championship rallying, Walter's development work on the turbocharged 4WD coupé was noted by Audi senior management. Walter Treser was appointed Audi Sport team manager. As such he was responsible for bringing the all-wheel-drive and turbocharging revolution to the classic rallies of the world, but his gallant service was brought to a halt by a fire on the 1981 Acropolis Rally. In June of that year he resigned from Audi Sport, returned briefly to Audi Research and Development and then quit Audi altogether.

Naturally his initial work outside the factory concentrated on Audi products. Working from the Ingolstadt area that is also home for Audi, he produced many special versions of the quattro. Particularly relevant to the development of the Treser roadster was an open version of the quattro, which was cumbersomely dubbed *Audi quattro Roadster von Treser*. About fifteen of these carefully designed convertibles were sold by mid-1985.

Below The novel Treser sportster comes in two versions, the convertible and the coupé shown here. Short it may be, and equally odd in appearance, but Treser has still managed to achieve an impressive drag coefficient

It was for this fresh-air quattro that Walter Treser created a glassfibre hard top which flipped beneath a protective rear deck lid. All the operator had to do was press two buttons. The system on the Treser roadster has been compacted and patented, so that the top rolls away behind the two seats and wastes much less space.

A methodical man, Walter Treser continued to produce alternative Audis while

Treser claims a maximum of 130 mph (210 kph) and acceleration from rest to 62 mph (100 kph) in 8.7 seconds . . . Fuel economy is exceptional for a 130 mph fun car . . .

progressing his two-seater design. From November 1983 to May 1984 he concentrated on building a three-dimensional model from the completed drawings. Apart from giving some solidity to Treser's creation this also allowed his employees to test the unusual shape in a wind tunnel. Despite a length of less than 160 inches an acceptable drag coefficient of 0.34 was achieved.

By October 1985 Treser had built a full-sized model of the car and had made some preliminary test runs. Minor restyling touches were added in May 1986. The final version was built on a comparatively long wheelbase of 98.4 inches (2500 mm) and is just 49.2 inches (1240 mm) high by 68.1 inches (1730 mm) broad.

Clever styling has made generous breadth versus compact length a virtue. Treser owners (whose number were set to swell after May 1988 when the car was to be produced at the rate of six per day) could feel they had bought something different, yet practical, in the fun car stakes.

Extensive testing began in April 1987. Venues included Volkswagen's own Ehra-Leissen, while intensive work was carried out at tyre manufacturer Michelin's southern-French facility

Not surprisingly the finished product uses Michelin TRX: 220/ 45VR-415 at the front and 230/

15VR at the rear. Incidentally those Treser 'Turbo' pattern wheels set something of a trend when they appeared on Walter's Audi conversions: the talented German engineer could claim to have inspired hordes of imitations.

A strong base on which to hang the plastic body was essential and Treser used a rigidly bonded 'AVUS' aluminium monocoque. Fitted with the ingenious two-seater body, the car weighs 2310 lb (1050 kg) and accommodates 15.8 gallons (72 litres) of lead-free petrol. The complete car has been fully tested by the strict German authorities, as were the special Treser quattro roadsters.

The running gear is based around four MacPherson struts and a quartet of servo-assisted and ventilated disc brakes. ABS anti-lock braking is an option and the strut suspension features the refinements of front and rear anti-roll bars with progressive rate miniblock springs.

The production engine and five-speed transaxle that sit ahead of and between the rear wheels, respectively, came from Volkswagen. In catalytic-convertor form, the double overhead camshaft, sixteen-valve four produces 130 bhp. This is less than a non-emission specification Golf GTi's 139 bhp, but performance and economy are still exceptional for a 1781 cc unit.

Treser claims a maximum of 130 mph (210 kph) and acceleration from rest to 62 mph (100 kph) in 8.7 seconds – very much on a par with the equivalent VW Golf GTi. Fuel economy is exceptional for a 130 mph fun car, ranging from 41.5 mpg at a constant 56 mph to 35.8 mpg at 75 mph and 24.1 mpg on the urban cycle.

Primary options on the well illuminated Treser (there are six forward halogen lamps) comprise air conditioning, leather upholstery, and power steering, but you can also have central locking, telephone, anti-theft alarm and six-speaker in-car entertainment.

Making its public debut some months ahead of production, Treser's promising design was premiered at the same 1987 Frankfurt Show as the Porsche Speedster and the similarly low-production BMW Z1. It is a measure of the respect accorded to Walter Treser that even in such company, he was taken extremely seriously. As he said to one German magazine, 'Enzo Ferrari was 48 when the first production Ferrari was made; I am only 47 . . .'.

Below It's hard to imagine from its purposeful appearance that the Treser is powered by only a VW GTI 16-valve unit. Thanks to its slippery shape and light weight, however, that's enough for a top speed of 130 mph

Above On the convertible the top retracts neatly into the cowling behind the seats – not as difficult as it at first sounds because, as the car's profile demonstrates, there is next to no top to retract

TRIKING

When you think of a car you naturally think of a vehicle with four wheels, but a car doesn't necessarily need a quartet of those circular devices. Several companies, not least Wolseley, have built two-wheelers in the past, but these have needed the complexity of gyroscopes to make them stable and have been short-lived as a result. This is not a problem that

G

afflicts three-wheelers, although they too, are usually dismissed as unstable. True, if a three-wheeler has the single support at the front it is quite likely to be lacking in stability, but if the lone wheel is at the rear, it is a completely different matter.

Morgan built three-wheeled cars for many years, first with a variety of motor-cycle engines but eventually with Ford four-cylinder power. Plenty of these have seen frantic action on Britain's race tracks, a sure sign that they are stable.

Although Morgan have long since gone the way of the rest and taken on a fourth wheel, there is still a car available which not only stays true to the tricycle theme but also revives the spirit of those classic bike-engined Super Sports Morgans.

Colin Chapman, legendary founder of Lotus cars, once said that if he were to build cars for fun and not profit then he would 're-invent' the Morgan trike, so it should be no surprise that it is one of his talented engineers who has, for a decade, got on with the job himself. Tony Divey lives not far from the Lotus factory and race shop up in Norfolk and his machine is called the Triking.

The Triking is really a three-wheeled motorcycle, in much the way that a Caterham 7 is a four-wheeled one, because it is built down to a weight level (a trifling 7 cwt – 355 kg) for maximum performance. So, the best bet for a light, yet powerful, engine would be an engine from a motorcycle, too, and of all the ones on offer, the engine which matches the style of the Morgans best is a longitudinal vee-twin, that is one with the cylinders splayed either side.

The Italian Moto-Guzzi concern has the perfect motor, in the shape of its 948 cc twin, which produces a useful 75 bhp. The unit may be a little lacking in the high-tech department, with its two pushrod-operated valves per cylinder, the design having been laid down in 1947, but it nevertheless provides the Triking with good acceleration. Bear in mind that with a driver on board and a little fuel, even 75 bhp gives a power-to-weight ratio of around 170 bhp per ton, which is as good as the Lamborghini Jalpa, for instance!

The Guzzi engine is air-cooled, so it sits at the extreme front, just as the JAP vee-twins used to on Morgans. There is no need for Mr Divey to worry about cooling, which helps to keep his machines light. Power is taken through the Moto-Guzzi five-speed gearbox, which is already attached to the motor, and onwards, via a prop-shaft to the Guzzi final-drive unit. With only one wheel at the rear, the design is again simplified, in that no differential is required.

The suspension aft is from the Guzzi, but at the front it is all original Triking, Tony using neat little twin wishbones with coil-spring/damper units slotted in. The main strength of the Triking is its central metal tub, to which a tubular front section is attached to hold the engine and suspension. The three brake discs are all foot operated (unlike the early Morgans which had pedals and a hand lever) and there is modern rack-and-pinion steering.

Below The problem with any three-wheeler that has the third wheel at the rear is styling the back successfully; Triking's solution is not the best thing about the car . . .

Right In complete contrast, the Triking viewed from the front is perfect, the Guzzi engine making it appear every inch a classic trike

AVF 353X

Left Powering the diminutive Triking is a thoroughbred among bike engines, the 948 cc Moto-Guzzi twin which produces more than ample power

Far left There may not be much of the interior but it's impeccably finished

The bodywork is a mixture of steel and glassfibre panelling and the whole is immaculately manufactured, as indeed you would expect of a car costing anything from £8000 upwards. Extras on top include leather trim, walnut dashboard, auxiliary instruments and weather equipment – although the Triking is not actually designed to be fully enclosed.

For those not used to a motorcycle gearbox, the Triking can cause a few problems because, unlike a car, it doesn't have a gate through which the gear lever can be slotted. Instead, it has a positive-stop system with first gear forwards and the following four all selected by a backwards pull on the lever, as if operating a ratchet. The problem is that you have to go through every gear, from fifth to first for example, and it is impossible to tell which slot you are in from the lever's position as this is always the same. Motorcyclists will find it easy (especially as there is still the neutral light on the dashboard to tell when no gear is engaged) and anyone will find it simpler than a car gearbox after a little practice, as it is certainly more positive.

For those who would rather not learn, however, and for those who live in Switzerland where regulations state that a car (no matter how many wheels it has) must have a reverse gear, Tony will attach a Toyota Corolla five-speed box; this naturally adds weight, but has another benefit in that the first and second gears are much 'shorter' than with the 'bike box which brings even sharper acceleration.

The Triking's narrow cockpit dictates that your right arm should hang out over the side; otherwise the three-wheeler feels just like any other open car – except on a smaller scale! Acceleration is excellent from the muscular big-twin: the Triking will probably manage 60 mph in under 8 seconds – and it will go on to a top speed of well over 100 mph, which is remarkable, bearing in mind that it is not at all aerodynamic. Progress, even on single-lane roads, can be very rapid because of the machine's diminutive size and even panic stops don't unsettle it much, because there is so little weight to pull to a halt.

The steering is as crisp as you would expect it to be, with the trike running on motorcycle tyres – the handling is neutral and the little machine can charge through corners. At the limit the whole vehicle slides and can easily be controlled in wonderful drifts, which makes the Triking one of the best fun cars around.

If the 948 cc engine isn't enough then you can specify Moto-Guzzi's 95 bhp Le Mans engine or you can wait until the company produces its four-valve versions, which will have more than 100 bhp! You can load your Triking up with as many luxury options as you can afford, but that is defeating the object a little. The car should be basic and, when it rains, you shouldn't be worrying about putting the hood up lest the leather get wet. You should get wet along with the Triking and let the water out later. It is much easier (and cheaper) simply to wear a rain suit and enjoy your 'Minimalist Morgan-style' motoring!

TVR

SEAC

The TVR 420 SEAC is one of the world's fastest convertibles; it has a claimed top speed of 165 mph and has already been raced to good effect, achieving results that have greatly encouraged demand for the car even though it costs almost £30 000. Yet many will be

wondering who is this TVR, and what does the SEAC designation stand for?

TVR is one of Britain's older specialist suppliers of sports cars, pre-dating the official formation of Lotus. Its forte today is lusty Rover V8 – and Ford V6 powered coupés and convertibles in sharply styled glassfibre.

In 1947 a twenty-three-year-old engineering enthusiast, TreVoR (hence the TVR initials) Wilkinson, decided to build his own sports car. The resulting alloy-bodied converted Alvis encouraged the construction in 1949 of the first tubular-chassis TVR.

That car joined a number of contemporary fledgling marques in Britain, most of whom struggled eventually into obscurity. For tax purposes, right up to the introduction of VAT, Britain differentiated between partly built 'kit cars' and completed cars, charging extra for the latter. This loophole encouraged an unusually high number of small businesses to attempt car

> *The most innovatory feature of the two-seater soft-top is the construction of the body in the Kevlar and Aramid composites that gave rise to the SEAC name*

Below The TVR 420 SEAC is powered by a Rover V8 engine which has been enlarged from 3.5 to 4.2 litres. Its 300 bhp gives the car true supercar performance

Above right Power is transmitted through ultra-grippy Bridgestone 225/50 tyres fitted to OZ spoke-style, split-rim wheels

manufacture, the most famous example being Lotus.

By the 1960s the features that mark out a TVR from the rest were quite plain. Those early Tuscan and Griffith models, powered by the American Ford V8, are resembled strongly by today's even-swifter V8 range.

Owners and managements have come and gone over the years, but TVR has remained loyal to its Blackpool base. Peter Wheeler bought TVR Engineering Ltd in 1980 and, in May 1987, acquired one hundred per cent control.

Peter Wheeler has always understood the importance of racing to the development, and establishment of a specialist

marque. The 420 Special Equipment Aramid Composite (SEAC) was developed on British race tracks before taking its place at the head of the TVR range. When it appeared for sale in October 1986, the SEAC commanded a £29 500 price tag that still applied in 1988.

The most innovatory feature of the two-seater soft-top is the construction of the body in the Kevlar and Aramid composites that gave rise to the SEAC name and boosted the price so dramatically over the £21 995 of the 390SE. TVR's own press release said: 'An overall weight saving of 200 lb is gained by the use of composite materials over a normally constructed vehicle'. The kerb weight quoted for the press demonstrator of 1987 was 'just 2300 lb (1045 kg), which compared with nearly 2500 lb (1136 kg) for the longer 390SE.

It is possible that the SEAC's extra aerodynamic equipment and bigger wheel/tyre combinations offset some of the low-weight construction gains. The car features a gently rounded

and extended nose section, flared wheel arches and an enormous rear spoiler, whose dished area extends beyond the back bodywork.

TVR's all-independent suspension system was substantially modified at the rear to cope with the 420's power capabilities. Braking echoes earlier Lotus and Jaguar practice: the 10.9-inch (277 mm) rear discs are located inboard, while the 10.6-inch (269 mm) ventilated fronts are mounted outboard and served by four-piston AP calipers.

Driving any of the V8-engined TVRs is quite an experience – there is just so much audible power – but the SEAC also generates astonishing track cornering forces on its standard 8.5 x 15-inch alloy wheels and Bridgestone 225/50VR rubber, which is of the RE71 type. Since customers can also plump for a massive 245/45VR-16 tyre on 9.5-inch-wide rims, TVR wisely

makes power steering available as an option.

Whether there has ever actually been a standard SEAC is open to question, since customers have been able to order virtually any power output they could afford and many other individual finishing touches besides. Handsomely trimmed, and having a comprehensive array of instruments and one of the fastest and neatest soft tops in the business, the TVR 420 SEAC is an exhilarating lesson in the right way to transfer track technology to the highway.

The SEAC's closest mechanical relative is the Blackpool company's 390SE model, itself a large-capacity version of the 3.5-litre, 350-badged Rover V8 TVR. In turn this descended from a Ford 2.8-litre (280) which debuted in the 1980 Brussels Show. All used a sturdy tubular-steel chassis and glassfibre bodywork, but the SEAC

The 420 SEAC's interior is sumptuously trimmed in piped leather and the dashboard features burr-walnut veneer; the telephone isn't standard

improved on that and introduced the public to the benefits of lightweight Kevlar coachwork and substantially modified aerodynamics.

During the 1980s, TVR gradually extended the power of the Rover V8 engine. At first it considered turbocharging the 2.8-litre Ford V6 that had served the company in so many previous applications (TVR offered a 230 bhp, turbocharged Ford 3-litre V6 in the late 1970s). Yet the comparatively fuss-free engineering and power delivery of the production Rover V8 won the day. And human nature being what it is, it was not long before the company began to extract more power from Rover's alloy 90-degree vee.

Today, TVR provides a choice of V8s: the 3.5-litre that has a fuel-injected 200 bhp (in the 350i), an over-bored 3.9-litre that generates 275 bhp for public sale in the 390

and the 4.2-litre for the 420 SEAC. This last unit has a bigger bore and longer crankshaft stroke than the 3.5-litre Rover V8's 88.9 x 71.12 mm. Replacement items that help provide 4228 cc via a 93.5 mm bore x 77 mm stroke include a steel crankshaft and 9.75:1-compression ratio Cosworth pistons.

Aside from the growth in cubic capacity, the extra horsepower can also be credited to a new camshaft profile and larger cylinder head valves. The valvegear is now operated by solid lifters and remains of the conventional pushrod type: this engine generates its substantial output by size rather than exotic engineering.

The SEAC V8 can be supplied with public-road output of 300 bhp at 5500 rpm, with 290 lb ft of torque, or for racing use with at least another 85 horsepower at extra expense. Even the comparatively mild 390SE, with its 275 bhp (also derived from a racing programme in the UK), is credited with a 150 mph maximum, so it is no surprise to find that TVR reckons on a maximum speed for the SEAC V8 of 165 mph and 0 to 60 mph in 5.0 seconds.

That is enough acceleration to get on equal terms with Aston Martin's considerably heftier 5.3-litre Vantage derivatives in all but outright maximum velocity. TVR's quoted power-to-weight ratio of 291 bhp per ton is better not only than Aston's Zagato (266 bhp per ton), but also than the Ferrari Testarossa and the Porsche 911 Turbo. Among current production cars, the SEAC beats all but the Lamborghini Countach's awesome 310 bhp per ton.

Above The profile of the SEAC is subtly different from its lesser stablemates as it features a deeper nose, full side skirts and a chunkier rear

Right The SEAC sports a massive table-like wing mounted on its boot lid which provides much needed stabilizing downforce at the high speeds which the Blackpool beauty can achieve

UVA

M6 GTR

UVA

The Unique Vehicle & Accessory (UVA) company has developed a four-wheeled answer to Road Runner, in the shape of a mid-engined two-seater that has an overall height of just 43 inches (1092 mm) and simply flies.

Power, masses of it across a wide engine rev range, is supplied by an enlarged, 3.9-litre, Rover V8 built by JE Motors at Coventry, the company that has provided power to the works Range Rovers in the arduous Paris–Dakar marathons. With this installed in a slippery coupé body weighing just 1725 lb

(784 kg), spectacular performance is guaranteed. More than 150 mph (241 kph) is on tap, complementing the swift 5.1-second time for the 0-60 mph (96 kph) sprint.

On road or track, wet or dry, this M6 GTR behaves impeccably and redefines the kit car as an honourable alternative to established 'off-the-shelf' products.

Newbury, Berkshire-based UVA is the brainchild of Alan Arnold. Initially the company dealt in the supply of off-road racers and parts imported from America, but now,

> *. . . the car's low weight and shapely
> lines ensure that performance will
> never be lethargic. All M6s share
> race-track handling, exciting style
> and braking ability*

though still serving that market, this small concern, housed in modern factory units, has graduated to the creation of its own structures and speed equipment. The striking M6 GTR is an emphatic statement of that self-sufficiency.

Cheaper versions of the UVA, with standard power outputs from 3.5-litre engines, as installed within the obsolescent Rover SD1, are also offered. That may mean less than 200 bhp, but the car's low weight and shapely lines ensure that performance will never be lethargic. All M6s share that race-track handling, exciting style and enormous reserves of braking ability.

Like Caterham Cars, UVA belongs to the SMMT specialist car group, and its products have been subjected to a ninety-one-point battery of German TUV tests. In the UK, kit prices start at £15 780 without VAT and the machine is also on sale in the USA.

By the summer of 1987, 23 M6 two-seaters had been made. The name acknowledges the debt owed by the low-line projectile to the McLaren M6 GT, a spectacular roadgoing development by the world-famous Grand Prix constructor of one of its racing cars.

Sadly, that original roadgoing Chevrolet V8 McLaren did not make even limited production, but the M6/M8 CanAm racers from the same concern continued to dominate that American category

Left Nestling behind the driver of the M6 GTR demonstrator is a tuned version of the ubiquitous V8 with the displacement increased to 3.9 litres

Above Dramatic styling to match equally dramatic performance, the UVA M6 GTR has it all

until Roger Penske/Mark Donohue and a very special Porsche 917 arrived to depose the British team. UVA's late-'80s interpretation of the M6 GT theme will ensure that the name lives on.

The design of UVA's composite seven-layer GRP (glass-reinforced plastic) monocoque chassis was begun in 1985. 'We chose such materials for the central cockpit/ tub and the body's six primary sections because we wanted to sell lightweight strength of an appropriately unique kind to the public', says Alan Arnold.

It was fun being introduced to the M6 at Donington race track in the sunshine. Having a background such as it does, it should be at home around a track, and, sure enough, it is. Giant 11-inch (280 mm) disc brakes at all four corners, a racer-like build and wishbone independent suspension, which needs no anti-roll bars, ensure inspired circuit manners. Mileage over rough roads quashes any reservations about the ride quality that such big wheels and tyres might provide. That carburetted 3907 cc V8 bellows as the car traverses the terrain, its chassis coping with awesome poise.

From adverse-camber B-roads in partial flood to a sunshine circuit at speeds which show that the 155 mph (250 kph) claim is no idle boast, is a fair test of any manufacturer's capabilities. And the results become even more impressive when it becomes clear that the constructor employs only eight people.

Released, the doors of the leather-trimmed cabin flip lazily but reliably upward. Are you really bold enough to slide inside? they seem to enquire. Lying inside on seating that adjusts through a Toyota/Ford-style air bladder, you feel that unforgettable motoring is undoubtedly in store, but will your view out be good enough fully to exploit the rumbling pleasure of 3.9 litres of aluminium Rover in a flyweight body? Although rear visibility is poor, forward vision is excellent and you do not notice the bulbous front wheel-arch contours once on the move.

The rebuilt aluminium Rover V8 engine behind the cockpit in the UVA demonstrator generates a rumbling 245 bhp to propel a weight just about that of a Metro. Spurts of the 248 lb ft torque were fed to acres of 50-series BFGs; the rears are 255 VRs on 10-inch rims,

Above left The instrumentation is comprehensive but UVA have lavished more attention on the M6 GTR's dynamics than its interior

Above Accessibility to the engine is almost easier than to the interior. Note how low is the steering wheel

the fronts only slightly slimmer at 8 inches across the beam. That such a power-to-weight ratio is effectively managed in foul weather over bumpy B-roads, says much for the conscientious development job UVA has completed.

Inevitably in a glasshouse like this, cockpit heat is a problem and the car is in need of better ventilation. Dramatic looks, which create an audience wherever the car goes, plus rattle-free delivery of power that copes happily with

town usage, warrants attention for a car that is sold in Britain in a kit form similar to that of the Caterham Seven – it is a straightforward job to complete construction on a DIY basis.

For overseas markets fully built cars can be supplied at extra cost. In 1987 thirty were ordered to fulfil an American contract, which could further establish this British company in the USA – rather ironic when you recall that UVA was established to import American specialist expertise.

The M6 GTR described would have cost 'about £18 000 complete and was designed to compete with the £28 000 Lotus Esprit Turbo,' says Alan Arnold. It lacks the racing pedigree and image of Lotus, but gives equally exciting, if different, driving pleasure. The abundant spread of power it has on call is more impressive than the Lotus, but its rearward visibility is poorer even than the rebodied Esprit. Nonetheless, this is a real budget supercar.

LM 164

WESTERN CLASSICS

The term 'kit car' has unfortunately become a generic description of a vehicle which isn't very well put together. However, out of the countless cars available for assembly at home, there are some which are at least as good as specialist production vehicles; the Classic Replicars LM 164 is one.

At first glance, a Ferrari *aficionado* would say that the LM 164 is a replica of the famous Italian 250 LM V12 racer that won the 1965 Le Mans 24-hour race in the hands of that unlikely duo,

Jochen Rindt and Masten Gregory However, the 164 emanates from Bradford-on-Avon, in the rolling hills of Wiltshire, rather than the famous factory behind the green doors in northern Italy's Maranello. And it isn't a replica. It is styled along the lines of the original, but every dimension is different and only from the front could someone easily confuse the two.

Even though the LM 164 now stands out as one of only a handful of truly good kit or component cars, it started from much humbler origins. A company in Dover called Rawlsons, who specialized in glassfibre work first decided to

build a kit car like the Le Mans winner and, as with many other kit-car and beach-buggy manufacturers, decided to use the venerable VW Beetle as base. The Beetle has a separate floorpan chassis, to which all its major components are bolted, and it is quite easy to take the VW body off and substitute whatever glassfibre confection on top you wish. The drawback is, of course, that you are left with a flat-four engine protruding from the rear – and no Ferrari has ever left Maranello with one of those!

Not surprisingly, with VW-powered kits available of just

about everything from Jeep to Lamborghini Countach, the Rawlson 250 LM didn't sell too well, but one man thought that it was a good enough idea to be developed. Mike Lemon of Classic Replicars redesigned the whole car around his own chassis and when Alan Frener, who now looks after the project came along, he decided that it needed 1980s power.

After considering the problem for some time, Alan thought that Ford would be the perfect answer; purchasing complete engine and transmission units from one of that company's special Power Product dealers, would give his cars proper warranty and thus make them more appealing to those *not* into D-I-Y. And Alan decided that a car that looks quick, ought to have the power to make it quick; thus he plumped for the Escort engine from the RS Turbo.

So, the LM 164 stands as a true mid-engined car, like the original, with the transversely mounted power train sitting behind the driver's shoulder. That most powerful of Escort variants is a healthy performer, too, with no less than 132 bhp and 133 lb ft of torque available from its 1597 cc. The alloy-head/iron block engine uses a single, overhead camshaft, Bosch KE-Jetronic fuel injection and a big Garrett T3 turbocharger with electronic engine management similar to that used on turbocharged Grand Prix cars. It comes with a five-speed gearbox and the whole assembly is bolted up into the 164's chassis, which is also equipped with modified Granada suspension at each corner. There was method in Alan trying to keep most service items from one parts bin: he wanted the car to be able to be maintained or repaired all around the world, an aim which would be easier to achieve if all the components likely to need attention were familiar to Ford dealers anywhere!

Unlike some manufacturers, Alan decided from the outset to build the LM up to a safety standard, not down to a weight limit, hence it is no featherweight, at just over 18 cwt (916 kg), but then as well as a fully triangulated 3 in (7.6 cm) steel-tubing backbone frame with perimeter

The interior harks back to the road-going Ferrari, with champagne-coloured leather seats edged in red piping to match the exterior

rails, the structure also comprises a steel floor and steel bulkheads fore and aft. With a hot turbo not far behind the driver, Alan didn't want to rely on glassfibre to keep out heat and noise. Glassfibre *is* relied on to clothe the beast, however, and Rawlsons still build the one-piece bodies.

The LM looks a lot smaller in real life than it does in photographs, but that makes it neither difficult to get into nor claustrophobic. The doors are large and open wide and the 'tunnel' separating the two seats is small, which leaves plenty of space for a solo driver. The interior harks back to the road-going versions of the original Ferrari, with champagne-coloured leather seats edged in red piping to match the exterior, while a purely British touch is the walnut-capping on the dashboard.

The LM will fit any driver under 6 ft (1.8 metres) like a glove (those over will feel as though they are in a very tight glove), and those lucky enough to drive will relish a car that is as practical as it is stylish. The view forward through the sharply curved windscreen (which comes from Marcos, just down the road) is excellent with those two curvaceous wings to help in guiding the car through tight gaps. Rear vision is good, too, for a mid-engined machine, with just the rear-three-quarter view demanding a little neck-craning

Top left & below left Certainly not your normal replicar interior, with wood veneer and wood-rimmed steering wheel; the Alfa badge is a little misleading, however . . .

Left The LM 164's mid-mounted Ford RS Turbo engine breathes through vents mounted above the rear wheel arches

on behalf of the driver.

Just as in many other mid-engined cars, the LM's gearchange isn't its strongest point and neither is the throttle linkage, which has quite a tortuous path from the driver's right foot to the fuel-injection system. The steering, though, is light and positive and guides the beast with real precision.

Alan Frener wasn't content just to use reliable Ford componentry for the suspension, but decided to call on experts to make sure that his car was well set-up. Hence he took a trip to yet another part of Wiltshire to visit suspension specialists, Geoscan, who set the LM up properly. Geoscan worked for many racing teams and have even helped F1 equipes in their time, so the LM 164 was no problem for them and their computer programme.

The result is a road car with track manners, albeit one which needs the utmost attention at all times on the part of the driver. The handling is crisp and accurate, but such is the sensitivity of the chassis that the LM needs to be driven positively: it is not a relaxing machine to drive quickly across country.

Power is there in abundance, and with rear-drive the LM has much better traction than the front-wheel-drive Escort, which enables it to reach 60 mph (96 kph) from rest in a little over 7 seconds (over a second better than the Ford) and then charge on to a top speed of 125 mph (200 kph). However, there is always a certain amount of throttle lag with a turbo engine and on the Ford unit this is particularly noticeable. That coupled with a precise chassis can make for sudden surges of power to transform the little car's handling from slight understeer to tail-out oversteer. Then the LM demands sharp driver reactions. A sweet-revving, free-breathing sixteen-valve non-turbo engine would suit the LM 164 much better.

Just about all the cars Alan Frener has built have gone abroad, as there appears to be more demand away from England for such a specialist car which retails for around £14 000 even before VAT has been added. Continuing interest and sales from countries as varied as Germany, America, Japan and Taiwan mean that the British are probably losing out somewhere. Much of it is probably down to the car being referred to as a 'kit': the LM 164 is too much of a thoroughbred to be labelled like that!

GLOSSARY

ABS Anti-lock braking system. A system where either an electrical or mechanical device prevents the wheels locking

Air dam A device attached to the front of a car below the bumper to limit the amount of air passing under the car and so decrease unwanted lift at the front and increase stability

Bhp Brake horsepower. A commonly used measure of engine work rate. Equal to 746 watts

Boxer A form of engine where the cylinders are horizontally opposed

Cd Coefficient of drag. A measurement of a car's aerodynamic efficiency.

CdA The Cd multiplied by the car's frontal area to give an overall air penetration figure

Carbon fibre Fibre used in a resin in the same fashion as glassfibre but giving a lighter and stronger material

De Dion A form of rear suspension which combines the precise wheel location of a live-axle system, the two wheels being connected by a rigid curved tube, with the lower unsprung weight associated with independent systems as the differential is not mounted to the axle

DOHC Double overhead camshafts. A form of valve gear used in high performance engines

Flat-four (-six, -12) Forms of horizontally opposed engine with four, six and 12 cylinders

Four-valve (quattrovalvole). A more efficient valve arrangement than the usual two per cylinder, allowing more mixture to be burnt by the engine

4WD Four-wheel drive

4WS Four-wheel steer

Group B The now defunct rally formula that spawned ultimate rally cars such as the RS200 and Lancia Delta S4

Homologation A system whereby the motorsport's ruling body lists certain cars or parts eligible for use in competition. Normally a certain minimum build number is specified

Kevlar A very strong composite plastic

Lb ft Pound feet, a unit of measurement applied to torque, or twisting force

LCD Liquid crystal display

Limited-slip diff A device used to prevent one wheel on a driven axle from spinning

Live axle A solid axle with centre differential and two drive shafts within the casing, a non-independent form of rear suspension

MacPherson strut A form of suspension unit whereby a strut

and concentric coil spring provide suspension and wheel location

Monocoque A form of car construction wherein the car's strength comes from the body rather than a separate chassis; it's now the standard form of construction

OHC Overhead camshaft

Polar moment of inertia A car's weight distribution. A design with a high polar moment has the weight biased towards the ends of the car (a Porsche 928 for example with front engine and rear transmission). A low polar moment model is usually mid-engined trading the extra stability of high moments for responsive handling

Spaceframe A lightweight form of chassis construction

Supercharger A device for forcing extra air and fuel into an engine to increase its power. Superchargers are mechanically driven

Spyder A convertible sports car

Torsen A form of limited-slip differential using worm gears. The name comes from TORque SENsing

Turbocharger A device for forcing extra fuel and air into an engine to increase its power. Turbos utilize the exhaust gases to drive a turbine, thus avoiding the mechanical drive of the supercharger

INDEX

ACKNOWLEDGMENTS

We are grateful to the following for their help with the photographs in this book:

The Patrick Collection (Aston Martin)
Brian Angliss (AC & Autokraft)
Audi Volkswagen (Audi quattro)
BMW (M3)
Jim Rooney (Chevrolet Corvette)
Callaway Engineering (Callaway Corvette)
Evante Cars
Maranello Concessionaires (Ferrari Testarossa)
Ford
Peter Thorp (Safir Ford GT40)
Performance Car (Lamborghini Countach)

Autocar (Lancia-Ferrari, Maserati Biturbo, Ferrari F40
Lotus Cars (Lotus Esprit Turbo)
Automobile (Ferrari F40)
Panther Cars
Peugeot
Porsche
Gerry Hawkridge (Transformer)
Tony Divey (Triking)
David Moore and Dave Haughin (TVR 420 SEAC)
Thomson & Taylor (Treser)
John Overton

SPECIAL PHOTOGRAPHY: Laurie Caddell